"Gentrification, spiritual l̲
ities and old dreams are
church and community. .
invested in both spheres, Mark provides in this book a mixture of
practical implementation, pastoral encouragement and theological
grounding for embracing our call to partner with Jesus in the transformative collisions between our church and our community."

Rick McKinley, lead pastor, Imago Dei Community, Portland, Oregon,
author of *Jesus in the Margins*

"Mark Strong is a pastor's pastor, and a deeply committed leader and
preacher. In *Divine Merger* he challenges us to do the spiritual work
of bringing our communities and our churches together. He does
this with wisdom and grace, inviting us to intentionally seek God's
leading for change for *both sides.* The book is inspiring, biblical and
practical. If you want to catalyze change in your church and community, this book, filled with stories of Mark's own experiences and
insights learned on the battlefront, can be a trusted guide."

MaryKate Morse, George Fox Seminary, author of *Guidebook to Prayer*

"Mark Strong is a legend in our city. The archetype of a wise, humble,
faithful urban pastor. Many younger planters look to him for more
than mentorship, but for a template to pour our own lives into.
When a guy like Mark talks about the collision of Jesus and community, I listen."

John Mark Comer, Bridgetown: A Jesus Church, Portland, Oregon

DIVINE MERGER

WHAT HAPPENS WHEN JESUS COLLIDES WITH YOUR COMMUNITY

MARK E. STRONG

FOREWORD BY KEVIN PALAU

IVP Books

An imprint of InterVarsity Press
Downers Grove, Illinois

InterVarsity Press
P.O. Box 1400, Downers Grove, IL 60515-1426
ivpress.com
email@ivpress.com

InterVarsity Press® is the book-publishing division of InterVarsity Christian Fellowship/USA®, a movement of students and faculty active on campus at hundreds of universities, colleges and schools of nursing in the United States of America, and a member movement of the International Fellowship of Evangelical Students. For information about local and regional activities, visit intervarsity.org.

Cover design: Cindy Kiple
Interior design: Beth McGill
Images: © Carther/iStockphoto

ISBN 978-0-8308-4452-4 (print)
ISBN 978-0-8308-9985-2 (digital)

Printed in the United States of America ∞

Library of Congress Cataloging-in-Publication Data

Names: Strong, Mark E.
Title: Divine merger : what happens when Jesus collides with your community /
*   Mark E. Strong.*
Description: Downers Grove : InterVarsity Press, 2016. | Includes
*   bibliographical references.*
Identifiers: LCCN 2015040191 (print) | LCCN 2015041774 (ebook) | ISBN
*   9780830844524 (pbk. : alk. paper) | ISBN 9780830899852 (eBook)*
Subjects: LCSH: Communities—Religious aspects—Christianity. | Evangelistic
*   work.*
Classification: LCC BV4517.5 .S77 2016 (print) | LCC BV4517.5 (ebook) | DDC
*   253—dc23*
LC record available at http://lccn.loc.gov/2015040191

P	21	20	19	18	17	16	15	14	13	12	11	10	9	8	7	6	5	4	3	2	1
Y	34	33	32	31	30	29	28	27	26	25	24	23	22	21	20	19	18	17	16

Contents

Foreword

Kevin Palau

I never get tired of talking about the encouraging things I see God doing in my hometown of Portland, Oregon.

Yes, that Portland. Home of the world's largest naked bike ride and the hit sketch comedy show *Portlandia*. First major US city to elect on openly gay mayor. One of the least churched and most politically progressive cities around. One of the least diverse major US cities. In the midst of (and perhaps partly because of) a context that some might find challenging to their faith, a group of pastors found each other. Maybe it was a sense of desperation. A realization that we need each other.

These leaders realized that if we were honest, our Christian community was known more for what we were against than what we were for. We had insulated and isolated ourselves—from each other and from the broader community. And this had greatly hampered our gospel witness. Could we recover a more biblical response? We realized we had never even met with our mayor to ask what we could do, collectively, to make a difference. How could we "seek the peace and prosperity of our city" together? We hoped to raise up fifteen thousand volunteers to serve that summer of 2008. To our great surprise, almost double that number—more than twenty-eight thousand folks from more than 400 churches—rose up and served in more than 380 projects.

My friend Mark Strong has been an instrumental part of this "Portland story," and now more than eight years into this relational movement we're seeing many encouraging signs. More than three hundred public schools in sixteen school districts in our metro area have formal church partners. Almost one hundred churches have banded together to collectively serve kids in foster care and those that serve them.

In the midst of the encouragement, Portland faces many issues. As in most major metropolitan areas, gang violence challenges some of our neighborhoods. When a spate of shootings rocked the city in 2012, mayor Sam Adams knew exactly what to do. He worked to convene the churches in the area to discuss what could be done. What emerged was an initiative called 11:45. Under the leadership of amazing pastors such as Mark Strong and George Merriwether, 11:45 sent out teams of residents, young and old, to walk hot spots identified by the police. The agenda was simple—just be a quiet presence, make friends, smile, shake hands, get to know people. Hundreds of people canvassed the area. And the result? Crime dropped dramatically. Gang activity was pushed out. The parks and streets became safe again. Shalom. Peace. Prosperity.

Divine Merger brings just the sort of theological reflection we desperately need to face the challenges of our day. When times are tough, when we feel we're losing our cultural influence and credibility, we always face several options. We can fight back harder, engaging in the kinds of culture wars that have branded us as primarily interested in "winning" and getting our way. We can retreat and isolate ourselves, to protect our kids and our churches from voices and influences we find distasteful or even offensive. We can give in, compromising to the point where the salt has lost its saltiness and there is no difference between the Jesus movement we belong to and the broader culture.

The great news, as Mark so ably points out, is that there is another, more biblical way to live and thrive. It's the way the church has always survived and even gained ground in the midst of the challenges it has always faced. It's the way of being in the world but not of the world. Of allowing the Spirit of Jesus himself, which indwells every Christ follower, to empower us to love in radical and creative ways that create curiosity in those we long to see come to faith in Christ. Mark lives what he preaches, and my prayer is that you'll allow this book to take you to a place of deeper love for our Savior and for the community all around you.

Introduction

Slowly and quietly speak these two words: "My community." Like a voice echoing in the Grand Canyon, allow the significance of these two words, "my community," to reverberate throughout your entire being. Through the echoes, reflect on the people you see and know in your community. Picture your family, your friends, the grocery clerk, the guy down the street, the school kids, the teenagers. Then focus on the injustices and hardships that make life difficult and even hopeless for those who are stuck in the margins of your community: the homeless, the elderly, the addicted and the abused.

Now stand, if you will please, over the same precipice, and shout these two words into the air: "My church!"

As these words echo, hear them not just with your ear but also with your heart:

- my church—a community of broken and dearly loved people who have experienced the transforming power of the gospel of Jesus Christ

- my church—a community that seeks to live in loving relationship with one another the way Jesus taught

- my church—a community glued together by the Holy Spirit

and equipped with incredible gifts and talents to serve one
another and our world

- my church—a community where hope lives, miracles happen
  and lives are transformed

- my church—a community that lives out God's mandate to be
  witnesses in our community of the power of the gospel of
  Jesus Christ to redeem and heal the lives of the broken

- my church—a community that is Jesus' physical presence in
  our community: his hands, his feet, his eyes and his heart

- my church—a community where God lives and is present

Now imagine this: What would happen if your church and
your community crashed in a head-on collision? You would have
exactly what God wants—*a divine merger*! A divine merger is
when the church intentionally integrates with its community.
When the house of God (your church) has a deliberate interaction with its community, the result is a kingdom transformation. What is a kingdom transformation? It's the meshing of
the earthly with the heavenly so that God's will can be done in
your community as his will is done in heaven. The beauty of a
divine merger is that Jesus himself orchestrates it so that *he* can
collide with your community and change it.

It's important to understand that your community needs the
church, and the church also needs the community. Satan's desire
is that the two never meet, but God has another plan: a wonderful, life-giving merger between your community and church.
He wants your community to meet his son Jesus and receive the
incredible love he has for them all.

God is extending an invitation for you to participate with
Jesus to forge a divine merger. It is not an invitation to change

the whole universe or make a mega-difference that costs millions of dollars. Nor is it an invitation to develop a sophisticated program that requires tons of machinery and oil to make it run. The invitation is *simply* a request for you to join hands with Jesus and make a collision at the spot in your community where he leads you.

The goal of this book is to help you get to that spot and to assist you in fulfilling your God-given mission in your community and church. My intention is not to force-feed you a particular model but to share some practical wisdom that can help any pastor, church leader or follower of Christ engage his or her community. Like you, I'm longing daily to see Jesus impacting the lives of those in my community. So we can learn together!

No doubt about it—your community is a prime place for a divine merger to happen. Even more importantly, your community is waiting for a life-giving Jesus collision. Like my high school football coach used to say, "It's time to get after it. Let's go!"

one

Strategic Positioning

I'm sure you've heard this before: "I was in the right place at the right time." Or maybe your ear has caught wind of another version: "I was in the wrong place at the wrong time." Note that in both cases, the speakers attribute the outcomes to chance.

Divine mergers require deliberate and strategic positioning. Meaning, by choice and by God's grace, you intentionally align yourself in a missional space between your church and your community. In other words, you constantly have one foot in the church and one foot in your community. When it comes to the church, you're all in; when it comes to the community, you're all in.

By living in this space, you can harness the capacity to facilitate a Jesus collision in your community. A vivid example that clearly defines the importance of strategic positioning is the life of Abraham.

Between Bethel and Ai

One verse has been extremely helpful to me and to our church regarding positioning: Genesis 12:8. The imagery in the verse illustrates the necessity of being in the right position. Not only that, it implies powerful prophetic possibilities and implications for our churches and communities. It says, "From there he went on toward the hills east of Bethel and pitched his tent, with Bethel on the west and Ai on the east. There he built an altar to the LORD and called on the name of the LORD."

Abram was having a fresh, life-changing encounter with God—an encounter that moved him out of his comfort zone and launched him on a God-guided journey into Canaan. The second stop of his journey is where Genesis 12:8 picks up. Since no Marriott or Hilton hotels are available, Abram has to pitch a tent. Where he pitches his tent is all-important. The location where he chooses to live for a season places him in a very strategic position.

The site of his lodging is between Bethel and Ai. To the west is Bethel, and to the east lies Ai. Absent from this verse are a few pieces of information that would be helpful to know. For one, it would be nice to know a bit about some of Abraham's interactions with the Canaanite people who were living in Bethel and Ai at the time. Also, it would be nice to have a footnote or two as to how Bethel and Ai acquired their names.

Many times in Scripture the names of individuals and places are based on their attributes. Bethel literally means "the house of God," and Ai is, by definition, "the heap of ruins." According to the literal meanings of these two cities' names, Abraham is living between the house of God and a heap of ruins. What a great snapshot of how to be positioned for a divine merger—living life between God's house and a heap of ruins!

You may not live in Canaan, but there is a Bethel and Ai near you. For us, Bethel is our local church. It is the place where we are in community with other Christ-followers. It is the place where Jesus Christ is celebrated and honored. It is the place where we grow in God's Word and in grace with others. Our Ai, on the other hand, is the community outside the walls of our local church. It is where the ruins of addiction, brokenness and hopelessness abound. It is the places where people who need Jesus live.

When we live life between our church and our community, we forge a unique paradox of missional tension. This tension from both sides creates a fulcrum that allows us to have a balanced ministry to our church and our community. That hallowed ground allows us the opportunity to feel the pull and calling of the church on one side and the pull of a community in need on the other side. That central position allows you to give each side equal value and equal commitment. Preferential allegiance to one side or the other is not a part of the equation. It is a package deal that calls you to live in a place where divine mergers can happen.

Jesus Builds and Loves the Church

The missional footprint Abraham leaves in the dirt is a great place for you to step into if you hope to position yourself to make a Jesus collision where you live. To make that step, it's crucial that you understand the importance of your local church. Jesus said to the apostle Peter, "I tell you that you are Peter, and on this rock I will build my church, and the gates of Hades will not overcome it" (Matthew 16:18). If nothing else, the church is important and has high priority because it is the single entity on earth that Jesus says he is building. Jesus doesn't say he's building a mall, a corporation or even a ministry; he's building his church. He's building the church to the degree that he will not allow the opposing forces of Hades to overcome it. The church will be built, and no force in the universe can stop it!

Jesus is building his church to fulfill his mission and purpose on the earth and, more specifically, in your community. The church is the instrument God is using to expand his kingdom on earth. That means if you are a part of the church, you are a part of the movement God is using to expand his kingdom where you live.

Jesus is not only the builder of the church; he is also the lover of the church. Sometimes I think we have no idea of the incredible love he has for his church. With all the church's imperfections, faults and quirks, Jesus is still madly in love with her. Unfortunately, people fall in and out of love with the local church all the time. The reasons for that lost love are as varied as the different types of cars on the road. Bureaucracy, egomaniac leaders, money issues, irrelevant values, broken trust, boring services, hypocrites—the reasons go on and on.

Let's be honest; no local church is a ten. I frequently say to our congregation, "No church is perfect. If our church used to be perfect, it was wrecked when I became the pastor and some of you became members." Everybody laughs and shakes their heads, but the statement is true. Our Redeemer is perfect, but the church still has a ways to go. The church is not Cinderella at the ball; we're more like Cinderella at home, living in the attic among the cinders, waiting in hope and expectation of her prince coming.

Yet you and I are still called to love what Jesus loves. He loves his church, and so should you and I. Living life in your local community of faith is necessary—even essential—and Jesus expects it of you.

Included in the missional footprint are not only your local church but your community as well. Let me float a claim here: No matter where you live—uptown, midtown or way downtown—

your community is in need of a Jesus collision. As long as a community isn't located in heaven, ruins are present somewhere.

Our church is in one of the hottest and fastest-growing stretches of real estate in the city of Portland. Phenomenal new buildings are being constructed around us, and fantastic new restaurants line the streets. Our community was listed as the number one destination for hipsters in the country. And the prediction is that thousands more will move in during the next few years.

As great as all that may be, we are still surrounded by ruins: broken families, violence, abuse, educational struggles, hunger and homelessness, isolation, mental illness—just to name a few. Where people abound, ruins abound.

All you have to do is take a good look; the ruins are present where you live. We can't bury our heads in the holy sand of church life and act as if broken people do not surround us. We have to be present. Like Abraham, we have to be in a location where the ruins of our community are in plain view.

The Challenge

Strategic positioning is easier said than done, because our natural tendency is to gravitate to one side or the other—the church or the community. While serving as a lead pastor since 1988, I've seen church leaders and laypeople alike become so absorbed in the community that they lose their focus and footing when it comes to life in the local church. Their loss of traction isn't intentional, nor are they church haters. Rather, they unknowingly fall into the vortex of community need and become consumed.

Sadly, I've seen many, though not all, suffer greatly in their spiritual lives due to being out of alignment. Their spiritual lives wane, and they become jaded and cynical toward the church. The church's lack of community concern and involvement doesn't sit well in their stomachs. The truth of the matter is that exposure to the ruins in one's community can be overwhelming, and the desire to make a difference can be all consuming, making it easy to get lost and drift away from the faith community.

I've seen others—myself included—become so entrenched in church life that our view of the community is eclipsed. The driving passion to fix and beautify Bethel makes it difficult to give attention to the community. We tell ourselves we'll get around to helping repair a few of the ruins in the community pretty soon. However, if we are out of position, there's a good chance that a divine merger will be only a passing thought and not a reality. The proverbial "I'm gonna ..." never gets followed through on. Sometimes it seems like we need an earthquake to dislodge both feet out of our churches so that we can get one foot into the community.

However, to move into the right position, you don't need an earthquake to jar you. All you need is an altar.

A Tent and an Altar

Abraham not only pitched a tent between Bethel and Ai, he also built an altar (Genesis 12:8). In Abraham's day, altars were significant and influential. The InterVarsity Press commentary on the Old Testament says this regarding altars:

> Altars function as sacrificial platforms. Their construction can also mark the introduction of the worship of a particular god in a new land. Abram's setting up of altars in each place where he camped defines areas to be occupied in the "Promised Land" and establishes these places as religious centers in later periods.[1]

In addition to these purposes, I want to emphasize here that an altar is a place of interaction between the God of heaven and a man or woman on earth. It's the meeting place where a merger is forged between the heart of God and the heart of the worshiper. The fact that Abraham pitched his tent between Bethel and Ai speaks powerfully of his geographical and physical positioning, but the altar shows that his heart is in the game as well.

Strategic positioning requires you to have your heart in the right place. Like Abraham, you can build an altar that gives a faithful testimony of Jesus Christ to your church and to your community. It goes without saying that your altar is not going to be made out of wood, stone and earth. It will be built with the materials found in a redeemed heart that is filled with God's love for his church and your community. Here are a few ways you can create an altar in your heart to anchor yourself in the right strategic place:

Allow God to capture your heart for your community. One of the most impactful stories I've heard of God capturing someone's heart for a community was told at a women's luncheon. I'm not sure why I was invited, but after hearing the message, I knew God wanted me to be there.

The speaker that day (I'll call him Joe) shared about how he ended up spending years serving in a small community in Mexico. An elderly missionary who served in that community had tried to convince him, almost to the point of nagging, that he should come and serve there. Joe refused the missionary's aggravating requests almost to the point of being rude.

However, after several months of going back and forth, they came to an agreement. The elderly missionary agreed to stop badgering Joe if he would just spend two weeks in the community. Joe agreed and made his way there. When he arrived, the only thought occupying his mind was *How can I make these two weeks go by fast so I can hurry up and get out of here?*

Nothing eventful happened during those weeks. Joe helped with a little work around the church, walked up and down the streets, talked with the people, ate a few tortillas and prayed a bit, and that was about the extent of it. Finally, it was time for him to leave. To say that he was thrilled to leave would be a whale of an understatement. He was extremely glad to be returning home and relieved that the days of harassment by the elderly missionary would cease.

When the missionary came to pick him up and take him to his bus, he said, "Why don't you ride in the back of the pickup so that you can say goodbye to everyone as you're leaving?" Joe obliged, and from then on it was "Home, James!"

As they drove down the road, he waved goodbye to the kids playing in the street and shouted, "See you later," to the men at the barbershop. He called out a few names of people he had met as he saw them walking down the street. He gave a hearty wave to the little grandma that had made him delicious tortillas. Finally, the community was no longer in his view.

As they left that little community, a God moment happened. Joe began to build an altar in the back of the pickup. Without warning, he began to sob uncontrollably, lamenting, "I cannot leave these people!" In those two weeks of exposure, unbeknownst to Joe, God had captured his heart for that community. He couldn't leave, because leaving those people would mean leaving his heart—and more importantly, God's heart.

He had built his altar between the church and the community. His position was secured, and he spent years serving and impacting that community for Jesus Christ.

You may not have an altar-building experience in the back of a pickup, but God can capture your heart for your community if you ask him and allow him to do it. God, in his wonderful mercy, can so fill your heart with love and compassion that you can't stay away from your community. Your miracle of heart is attainable! He will meet you right where you are now, pickup or no pickup.

Embrace a theology that requires a community witness. Jesus makes it unmistakably clear that the church is called to be a witness to its community. The call is grounded in what he says we are: the salt of the earth and the light of the world. In Jesus' mind, the essence of who we are determines our function, opportunity and responsibility. He says,

> You are the salt of the earth. But if the salt loses its saltiness, how can it be made salty again? It is no longer good for anything, except to be thrown out and trampled by men.
>
> You are the light of the world. A city on a hill cannot be hidden. Neither do people light a lamp and put it under a bowl. Instead they put it on its stand, and it gives light to everyone in the house. In the same way, let your light shine before men, that they may see your good deeds and praise your Father in heaven. (Matthew 5:13-16)

Both salt and light in this context are powerful metaphors of how the church influences the world, which includes your community.

Salt and light combat the decay and darkness prevalent in all communities. As salt, we are God's preservative in places where lives are being ravished by the decay and erosion of sin. Being salt, we are also an antiseptic to be applied to the painful wounds inflicted by injustice, the hands of careless individuals and the adversary. We are also flavor enhancers, gifts of God's grace to souls who dine continuously on the bitter herbs of sorrow.

We are light, emissaries of radiant hope who declare to a dark world that there is a God who loves them. We are light, illuminating the way for others to find life and life more abundant in Jesus Christ. We are light, purifying beams of God's love that expose sin—not to shame but to redeem and restore. We are light, desperately needed to expel the darkness in our communities.

To paraphrase, Matthew 5:16 concludes with Jesus saying, "Be what you are and do what you have been created to do." Be the salt in your community and let your light shine brightly so that people can see an expression of God through your life and glorify him as a result.

If we are followers of Jesus, adherence to this truth is not open for negotiation. We are a city on a hill for everyone to see, and our lights are not to be hidden. Our response should be to embrace the call and to be obedient to the purpose of the Master. Dietrich Bonhoeffer said, "Flight into the invisible is a denial of the call. A community of Jesus which seeks to hide itself has ceased to follow him."[2] That's not us! We embrace the call to be salt and light, and by doing so, we position our hearts for Jesus collisions to happen all over our communities.

Discern in your heart the will of God. I thoroughly enjoy listening to congregations' stories and hearing about the various ministries going on in churches. Recently, at a church in San Jose, California, where I preached, I asked the pastor to take me on a guided tour since I always love touring church facilities to get new ideas for our church. After we had seen a number of the rooms, Pastor David walked me into their youth/children's area. In that room were a good number of people who, according to Pastor David, were not members of the church. The people present were members of the community who had come to the church to throw a rowdy yet civilized birthday party for a young child.

This party looked like one my wife and I would throw at Chuck E. Cheese's for our kids—except that it was in the church, hosted by members of the church for community members who did not attend the church. There were all sorts of games and other fun things available for the kids to enjoy. The atmosphere was clean, safe and festive. Not only that, but the parents seemed to be having a good time too.

A young woman in the church had a burden to engage her community and felt in her heart that this was what God wanted her to do. The idea was genius! Throughout the year, hundreds of people come and have kids' parties at the church. While there, they encounter Jesus through the loving people who are present not only to give them a good party but also to express God's love tangibly to them. As a result of this community ministry, some have come to faith in Christ, and a link to the church has been established so that if one of the families has a crisis or need, they know where they can turn.

This ministry brings Ephesians 5:15-17 to life: "Be very careful, then, how you live—not as unwise but as wise, making the most of every opportunity, because the days are evil. Therefore do not be foolish, but understand what the Lord's will is." This young woman was able to position herself because she knew in her heart what God was asking her to do, *and she did it.*

Live to worship God. You can't have an altar without a sacrifice. Jesus is the ultimate sacrifice for us; he has already paid the price for us by giving his life. However, each of us can also offer our lives to God in love, adoration and service toward him.

I heard a story about a little boy who wanted to give God an offering but had nothing to give. He sat on the floor, watching people pass by and place their offerings in large wicker baskets. How he longed to give a little something to the Savior he so dearly loved. He walked to the front of the church, grabbed the rim of the basket and hoisted himself inside. When the deacons went to retrieve the boy, one scolded him, saying, "This is not a play area!" Embarrassed and bewildered, the little boy responded, "I didn't have anything to give the Lord, so I was giving him myself."

The altar of our heart is where we can put our entire being in the offering basket and say to the Lord, "Jesus, I am giving you all of me." Out of that loving surrender to the Master, God can put your life in the place where you are supposed to be. Romans 12:1-2 tells us how to climb into the basket:

> Therefore, I urge you, brothers, in view of God's mercy, to offer your bodies as living sacrifices, holy and pleasing to God—this is your spiritual act of worship. Do not conform any longer to the pattern of this world, but be transformed by the renewing of your mind. Then you will be able to test and approve what God's will is—his good, pleasing and perfect will.

My friend Dewitt Jones wrote the song "Use Me," which was popular way back in the 1990s. One line went like this: "If You can use anything, Lord, You can use me." Friend, you are not just *anything*, you are *something*. As they say in the country, "You're something mighty special!" So, what are you waiting for? Climb in the basket and offer yourself totally to God by worshiping him with all you are. He will use your life beyond your wildest dreams and imaginations.

Be practical. You have essentially three gifts to offer to your church and your community: your time, your talents and your treasures. Your time is the hours you have during a day. Your talents are the abilities and gifts God has equipped you with to serve others. Your treasures are your finances and other resources God has placed in your hand. Positioning yourself correctly in a practical sense requires you to allot the use of your time, talents and treasures in a way that they are distributed to your church and your community adequately.

Pitch Your Tent

Abraham pitched his tent and built an altar between Bethel and Ai. In our time, that is the same as being strategically positioned between the church and the community. So, like Abraham, pitch your tent between the two. Make the effort and the choices that will drive the tent stakes deep and anchor you in a missional place. Build your altar to allow the Spirit of God to capture your heart for the people around you. Your community is waiting for life-changing Jesus collisions to happen.

God is ready to use you to forge a merger where you live. It won't happen by chance, but it will happen if you are in the right position.

What's your location?

For Reflection and Discussion

1. Where are you located position-wise between your church and your community?

2. What challenges make it difficult for you to be positioned correctly between the church and your community?

3. Why do you believe it's important to have a right theology about the church's responsibility in the community?

4. Has there been a time when God has captured your heart for your community? Explain.

5. How will you endeavor to build an altar in your heart between your church and your community?

6. How will you pray for yourself and your church's missional position?

two

Break Out

The nineteenth chapter of the book of Judges contains one of the most repulsive and heartbreaking stories in the Bible. If this tragic chapter were a film, the review might read something like this:

> *Unbelievable* is a film adaptation of a true story that graph-ically illustrates the dark side of human nature, the erosion of moral values and the terminal sickness of a godless culture and community.
>
> The plot centers on a married couple experiencing deep-seated chronic issues. Hammer, the husband, has always treated his wife with contempt, viewing her and treating her as a second-class citizen. Over the years, his lack of respect and unloving behavior has beaten her self-worth out of her heart and soul.
>
> Rachelle, the wife, complicates the marriage in her own way. It's unclear whether she has been maritally unfaithful to Hammer, and in a fit of anger, she leaves him and re-turns to her father's house, fragile and broken. After four months, Hammer realizes she's not coming back, so he journeys to her father's house to persuade her to return home with him.

It's clear that her father is not enthused about his daughter leaving, so he uses every tactic he can contrive to delay their departure. After several days, Hammer has had enough, and they leave at dusk.

The lateness of their departure makes it necessary for them to find lodging for the night. They pass through a couple of towns but opt not to stop. Their goal is to reach a certain supposedly God-honoring city, which they think will be welcoming.

Upon their arrival, they discover the opposite; they are left to spend the night in the city square in need of food and rest. Fortunately, an elderly gentleman from a neighboring town sees them as he returns home from working in the city and welcomes them into his home. And the *unbelievable* begins.

Everyone is settled into the home, and they're enjoying a good meal and conversation when a loud banging on the door startles them. Pounding on the door is a group of wicked men who demand that the old man send Hammer outside so they can sodomize him. In an effort to defuse the situation, the old man goes outside and attempts to reason with them, asking them not to perpetrate such a vile act.

Equally as immoral is the solution he offers: his own daughter and Rachelle as objects to appease their gluttonous sexual appetites. Hammer thrusts Rachelle out of the house into the pit of wolves. Tragically, they rape and abuse her all night.

Early that morning before daybreak, Rachelle takes the last steps of her life. She manages to make it back to the home where her husband is staying. But, abused and broken, she falls down at the door and stays there until daylight.

That morning, as Hammer leaves the house, he steps on his wife. Callously, he says to her, "Get up. Let's go." But there is no answer. His wife's cold body lies at the door, her hand clutching the threshold.

Hammer places his wife's body on his donkey and takes her home. Instead of giving her a proper burial, he cuts her body into twelve pieces and sends the parts to the twelve tribes of Israel. A civil war breaks out, and twenty-five thousand men in the city where Rachelle was murdered are killed.

Whenever I read this passage, I'm overcome with two powerful emotions. The first is intense anger. As a pastor, I probably shouldn't say this, but the chapter arouses anger in me to the point that I wish I could have been Bruce Lee for about thirty minutes that night and have a good crack at all those despicable men—Hammer and the old man included. I'd unleash on each one of them a full repertoire of kicks, guttural screams and karate chops. They would learn firsthand the meaning of nunchuck. Can you feel me?

Even stronger than the anger is the sadness I feel for the abused woman in the story. For a person who is made in the image of God to suffer abuse to that degree breaks my heart. It's not right. It shouldn't have happened at all. I can't help but weep. What a tragedy!

Meet Them at the Threshold

If I weep over a story of injustice that occurred several thousand years ago, how can my heart not be broken by the abuses and needs that people in my community suffer every day? How can

I not be concerned? Look at Judges 19:27: "There lay his con-
cubine, fallen in the doorway of the house, with her hands on
the threshold." Here's the reality: This woman died with her
hands on the threshold of the door. She was so close, yet so far
from receiving the help she needed to live.

In your community right now and every day, people are col-
lapsing and hanging on to the threshold for dear life. The forces
that drive them to that place are numerous. Forces such as sex
trafficking, hunger, drug addiction, racial prejudice, unem-
ployment, broken relationships, poverty and fear shove those
whom God loves to their knees and say, "You die here!" These
people are hurting too badly to scream for help, and in some
cases they have given up hope of ever finding the oxygen they
need to live. They are gasping for air at the threshold, hoping
someone will come very soon.

Brenda, a woman who came to faith in Christ at our church,
told me the story of how she almost died at the threshold. She
had grown up in a respectable family and never wanted for anything. Along the way, she hit some bumps in the road, and she
ended up associating with some bad characters. You can probably
figure out the progression of this story. She became strung out
on drugs to the point that no one in her family would have
anything thing to do with her.

As a result of her addiction, she lost every possession she had,
except her car. For months on end she was high, living in her car
on the street behind our church. Her physical presence was frail
and emaciated, her health jeopardized, and she was alone.

Brenda cried out to God for help, and people from the church
reached out to her. By God's grace and through his church, a
Jesus collision happened and a merger went down, allowing her
to live instead of dying on the threshold.

Brenda's story turned out fine because she was reached in time. But what about all of the other Brendas in your community who are clinging to life, holding on to the threshold? They're waiting for you to break out.

Breaking out is not a heroic or grand-scale event, nor does breaking out require you to be a spiritual giant that can move mountains. It isn't the result of a super-spiritual experience either. *To break out of the four walls of your church and into your community, you simply step outside the door and help minster life to the person or persons in your pathway.* You open the door and extend to your community the gift of God's grace.

Come on, church! We cannot afford to stay asleep in the house while the people that God loves are right outside the door, perishing. Let's meet them at the threshold. It's time to open up the door and take the steps to make a Jesus collision in your community. If the door won't budge, break out the WD-40 and lubricate the hinges; we simply can't afford to stay inside.

To open the door, we must identify why they remain closed, so what follows are a few things that keep us inside.

Lethargy

Let's not pull any punches here. One of the reasons we are behind the doors of the church is spiritual lethargy. Living our lives in a toxic fog of personal concern, religious activities and pleasurable pursuits slowly lulls us to sleep. The fog allows us to live our lives oblivious to the issues that are affecting the community around us.

The men in Judges 19 lived in the fog of an immoral culture. How else could they give their womenfolk over to be abused— then sleep in the following day? Have our churches been so lulled to sleep by our culture that we ignore the people dying on our doorsteps too?

In my first years of pastoring Life Change, our church was asleep—sound asleep! We didn't talk about evangelism; there was no outreach to the community. We were without a doubt in the fog, fast asleep. Our only concern was for God to keep on blessing our little church.

In my frustration, God gave me an idea. The Lord spoke to my heart and told me to take the community to my congregation. Now, this was before the world of digital cameras, LCD projectors and PowerPoint. So I grabbed my 110 Kodak camera and took pictures of our community. I took shots of people struggling in life, shots of rough places in the community, shots of neighbors who lived next door. You name it, I photographed it. After finishing my photo shoot, I took the film to the photo shop and had them make slides so I could create a slide show.

That Sunday we flipped the script on how we conducted our church service. I asked everyone to get comfortable and told them we were going to watch a home movie via slide show. We viewed and talked about each slide, and when it was all said and done, our church had been exposed to our community.

I can't say that after that cinematic experience we arose like a mighty army and conquered our community. However, I can say the church woke up. We actually began to dialogue about the problems in the community and discuss what we might do to help. Our prayers changed from asking God just to bless our little church to asking him to bless our little community. We also began to take baby steps toward engaging our neighbors.

It helped to set the trajectory for all that our church is doing in our community today. The Lord used that pitiful slide show to splash cold water in the face of a church he loves so it would reach a community he loves. We were finally awake.

A Faulty Premise

Lethargy is a barrier, but so is a faulty premise. I'm a pretty avid football fan. Having grown up in Bellevue, Washington, and Portland, Oregon, my two favorite teams are the Seattle Seahawks and the Oregon Ducks. Every year I'm pulling for the Hawks to win it all and for the Ducks to be victorious. Over the last couple of years, both of my teams have had great seasons. The Hawks made it twice to the Super Bowl, and the Ducks were one of the first two college teams to play in the inaugural BCS College Championship.

Even though I'm rooting for my teams to bring home the championship trophy, it's not going to happen every season. In the 2014 season, the Ducks failed to win the big one, but they still played great, entertaining football. Losing that game doesn't mean the team was a bust.

Many times we approach ministry with the expectation that we're going to bring home the trophy in everything we do. This means that if we're working to reform foster care, we fail unless we change the entire system. If we're working to stop gang violence, success means another violent crime never happens. If we're serving homeless youth, we miss the mark if one youth is still sleeping on the street. I've been there before, and I still occasionally drift back into the paralyzing premise that says, Unless what I do totally fixes the whole problem, why do it? In other words, if what I can offer is so small, why bother?

A lot of us are honest enough to admit that no matter what we do, the problem is not going away. And sadly, our honesty is enough to let the air out of our balloon. Knowing that the issue will never completely go away, we do nothing. We stay behind the closed door, separated from the soul who is gasping for life at the threshold.

God is not interested in you winning championships, nor does he see your small offering as nonessential. His definition of success is you being faithful and obedient to do what he asks of you, day by day, week by week, month by month and year by year. In your faithfulness, you are watering and planting the kingdom in the life of your community by fulfilling your assignment. Like the mustard seed (see Matthew 13:31-32), your influence will grow, people will move closer to God, and divine mergers will happen. From that small seed, terrific miracles will bloom. Understanding this frees us from the notion that we have to fix the whole problem and that nothing you or I can contribute makes any difference. No, we are called simply to water and plant, and God will make it grow. You and I just have to step outside the door and be faithful.

Oh, and for the record, you are a part of a championship team called the church, and your team captain is Jesus, the undisputed champion of the universe. So go ahead; open the door and step out. You and Jesus will make a difference.

The Enormity of the Problem

Cousin to having a faulty premise is being overwhelmed by the enormity of the problem. You desperately want to engage your community, but the problem is so massive you don't know where to start. You end up at a stalemate because you don't know how or where to move.

As we stood in the foyer one Sunday after church, my friend shared a story with me that drives the point home. Her little niece had succeeded in ransacking her bedroom from top to bottom. The darling had managed to unmake the bed, pull all her clothes out of the closet and drawers, and empty out her toy box. In essence, her floor was filled with mounds of debris.

When her mother walked into the room, she instantly suffered an acute form of oh-my-Lord parental shock. She thought, *Are my eyes playing tricks on me, or is this room a natural disaster?* Composing herself, she did the logical parental thing and told the little girl to clean up the room immediately.

After an hour or so, she heard her daughter sobbing profusely, so she went back upstairs to check on her and see how the cleaning was progressing. When she peered into the door, the room was in the same state of emergency. Ignoring the mounds of clutter, the mother asked, "What's the matter?"

The little girl said, "I can't, I can't . . . too much, too much!" The mess in her room had overwhelmed her. She didn't even know where to start.

The mammoth needs and complex issues that pervade your community can cause you to experience the same paralysis as that mother. You are surrounded by so much community debris that you find yourself frustrated and at a loss for where to begin.

To be honest, there are times when I feel just like that little girl. I've had long stretches of time when I felt emotionally, spiritually and psychologically overwhelmed. Not knowing where to start or what I should do, I've sat in my office, scratching my head and asking the Lord, "What in the world do you want me to do?" On numerous occasions, I've left my office more frustrated than when I entered, because the more I thought about the situation, the more my heart said, *It's too much. It's too much!*

I wish I could give you a deep, insightful, prophetic prescription to remedy this. But the answer is simple. It's *super simple.* Reach out your hand and start picking up one thing at a time. For example, if you have a heart to help children in your community, go to the elementary school down the road and volunteer for an hour or two a week. Help teach the kids to read or, if you like to walk around, volunteer to be a lunchroom monitor. The children and staff could grow to love you, and you could make a difference in your community.

Mrs. Jan runs a drop-in center for kids at a high school in our community that has seen some very rough days. The school gave her a room, and she has been instrumental in remodeling into a cool space where students can hang out. They drop by during the day to relax, do homework, talk and eat. Mrs. Jan is retired and could be off enjoying her children and grandkids in a much warmer climate than Portland. However, her passion is for those high school kids. She loves them and desires to see them succeed in life.

A year or so ago, Mrs. Jan told me she was going to take a break. There was too much stuff to deal with at the school. She wasn't volunteering to slog through a political quagmire and other adult issues, but simply to help the kids, so she made the decision to back off.

Several months into her respite, the yearning for the kids wouldn't subside, so she made the decision to focus on the one thing that motivated her and pulled at her heart: the kids. She took her attention away from trying to fix and figure out all of the surrounding issues in need of repair and placed her focus on the kids. Now she's back at it and is continuing to make a big difference in the lives of kids at our local high school.

Your church has been ordained by God not to sit and cry in the middle of the floor but to work with him in cleaning up the messes and spills where he has placed you in—your community. Start by picking up one thing at a time.

Fear

Fear is a powerful, paralyzing force that can prevent you from turning the knob on the door and walking out to the threshold. Here's a simple acrostic that defines fear: false evidence that appears real. How many of us are boarded up inside our church walls because of a boogieman? True, there are legitimate concerns when engaging a community, but in most cases they are few and far between. Many of our fears are founded on our insecurities, inadequacies and ignorance. In truth, most people are longing for a divine merger, and they appreciate when you share God's love with them.

God has given me the gift of evangelism. In our community, I've shared the gospel individually with hundreds of people. Having gospel conversations with those around me is one way God has shaped me to facilitate Jesus collisions in my community. However, just because I know what God wants me to do and that he's given me a gift doesn't mean it's always easy. I have to fight fear constantly!

Though I struggle, a situation I experienced in college helps me to keep the fear monster in check. I was sitting in a speech class at Portland State University when about halfway through, the Lord began to speak to me concerning an older woman in the class. As plain as day, I heard the Lord say, "Tell her that I love her." For forty-five minutes I sat in my chair having a no-holds-barred wrestling match within my heart. I thought to myself, *There is no way I'm going to go up to this total stranger and tell her Jesus loves her.* For one, she looked like one of those people who would tell you a few choice words about God, Jesus and the Bible, and that particular day I wasn't up to a bowl of conflict and a cup full of rejection.

When class was dismissed, she went her way, and I went mine. Out of sight and out of mind—at least until the next day of class.

Sitting in class the next day, I was relaxing in a place void of any internal spiritual conflict when I heard the same voice I had heard two days before: "Mark, I want you to tell that woman that I love her." This was starting to get a little strange, because there were ten minutes left in class, and the woman wasn't even there. But about five seconds after the Lord spoke to my heart, in she walked. With ten minutes left, she had come to class. By now the fear of God was on me, so I knew I had to swallow pride and fear and tell this woman Jesus loves her.

Class was dismissed and, like a coward, I walked up to her and said, "My name is Mark, and I'm not trying to destroy your day, but I feel like God wants me to tell you that Jesus really loves you." What happened next was incredible. In the middle of the hall, with hundreds of students walking by, this woman practically dropped all of her books. She cupped her hands together and held them to her heart. With eyes as bright and wide as seashells, she blurted out, "Oh, he really loves me!"

I said, "Yes, he does."

She began to tell me her story. She had been involved in a terrible car accident that almost ended her life. For some reason unbeknown to her, she had survived. She said she had never heard about Jesus before she picked up a wet tract off the curb of a street one day, and the information on that tract was all she knew about Jesus Christ. I had the opportunity to be the first person to tell the story of Jesus and his love for her. She didn't have bad words to say about God, nor did I get a bowl of conflict or a cup full of rejection. She was extremely grateful for the Jesus collision in the hallway that day, and so was I.

We never know how God has prepared the way for us to serve in our communities. Fear tells us to stay out, but God says, "Fear not! Go and make a merger!"

Resources

Another door closer that can prevent you from breaking out into the community is the fallacy that you don't have enough resources to make a difference. You can't let a lack of resources keep you from doing what God has called you to do. Where God guides, he provides. That may sound cliché, but it's true. God's track record is solid; we see his provision for his servants in Scripture. Likewise, if you go, you will see his provision for you in your community.

Phil has had his share of struggles. He doesn't have a lot of money, and his personal living condition presents a real challenge for him at times. But he loves Jesus, the church and people. For a number of months, Phil had a burden for the growing homeless population in our city. He would approach me after our worship services and talk to me about how he felt God wanted him to do something with the homeless population.

He started to give the homeless people he saw a sandwich or two whenever he could. Now, months later, he has a number of great relationships with some members of the homeless community. Every week, they come over to his house to make sandwiches and serve the people on the streets together. These wonderful souls are meeting not only Phil, but also Jesus.

Phil allowed Jesus to use him to facilitate a merger. Even though he was struggling financially himself and lived in a difficult place, he went with what God put in his heart, and God has faithfully met the needs along the way.

Here's a great promise for you if you are in need of resources and provision to carry out your assignment: "And God is able to make all grace abound to you, so that in all things at all times, having all that you need, you will abound in every good work" (2 Corinthians 9:8).

The imperative word here is *all*. In all things, at all times and in all that you need, God is able to bless you to excel in every good work. Therefore, focus less on what you need and more on God's willingness and ability to provide for you. Be confident that in every step you take he can supply all you need.

Satanic Resistance

Almost three years ago, in conjunction with our district attorney's office, the Portland Police, the City of Portland and a few of the judges in our court system, a group of us pastors started the Family Mentoring Program. The judges and DAs were discovering that young men from ages eighteen to twenty-six were being arrested and sentenced for low-grade misdemeanor crimes. These young men had not yet perpetrated crimes that would force them to do significant prison time, but if there were no intentional intervention, many would eventually end up in prison.

After several months of discussion and figuring out how the process would work, we came up with a plan. Our strategy entailed using the court system not just for punitive purposes but also for redemptive opportunities. According to the program, when a young man who fit the legally prescribed criteria stood before the judge, part of his bench probation would be to meet with a mentor. The mentor would make contact with the young man, take him out to lunch, listen to his story and educate him on resources available to help him succeed in life. In addition, the mentor would leave the door open for a deeper relationship if the mentee desired. The mentors at the time were all pastors in the community who personally wanted to fill a great need in our community.

We had been underway for several months and had come into contact with some young men in desperate scenarios. One that I spent time with was living in a two-bedroom apartment with his uncle and several other people. He was estranged from his biological father, and his mother was engrossed in her struggle with drug addiction. Not only that, but he also had eleven brothers and sisters living in dire straits.

Another young man we mentored ended up getting shot on the street behind our church. The wounds he sustained almost ended his life right there, but Bishop Pollard, his mentor, happened to be driving by. He got out of his car and saw the young man he had been spending time with dying on the ground. Bishop said the first responders were about to give up trying to resuscitate him. Sobbing, he prayed and encouraged them to keep trying. Finally, the young man coughed, and they were able to get him to the hospital. After a number of weeks, he made a full recovery.

I could tell you a number of other stories about some of the young men we have worked with, but the fact of the matter is that they live in our community, and they desperately need some positive role models, hope, and most of all, Jesus!

In my opinion, anyone would see this service to these young men as necessary and needed, right? Wrong!

Somehow our program caught the eye of some local media and eventually a national religious watchdog group out of Washington, DC. I was floored when I heard a national talk show host blasting the city for giving money to pastors to take criminals out for lunch. It took me a minute before I realized he was talking about *our* program. Due to all the media, and more specifically the dust stirred up by the watchdog group, we had to put the program on hold. Sadly, the young men got the raw end of the deal, as in other areas of their lives.

When you or I engage our community on any level, we have to recognize that we have an adversary that absolutely does not want a divine merger to happen where you live. Your primary goal is not only to help someone have a better life. Your service to your community is ultimately about communicating God's eternal love and plan to people who desperately need to know Jesus Christ as Savior and Lord. That being the case, Satan will fight tooth and nail to keep your mission from being accomplished.

I've heard some people accuse Satan for everything under the sun. Whenever a difficulty arises, they blame it on the devil. On the other hand, there's the camp that dismisses his existence and activity in human affairs. Both views are incorrect. In reality, Satan is not the cause of all difficulty and evil, but neither is he nonexistent. The Bible teaches us he is an adversary who opposes God's purposes. Also, he's the prince of this world and seeks to destroy the shalom that God wills for all of humanity.

The apostle Paul explains to the Thessalonians that his failed attempt to see them face-to-face was due to Satan blocking the way: "But, brothers, when we were torn away from you for a short time (in person, not in thought), out of our intense longing we made every effort to see you. For we wanted to come to you—certainly I, Paul, did, again and again—but Satan stopped us" (1 Thessalonians 2:17-18).

Satan blocking the way implies that he is attempting to hinder or prevent the accomplishment of your intended goal.

Satan will use people, policies, pain, pennies and problems to prevent you from breaking out and accomplishing the service God has called you to fulfill. That's what happened to our program. He tried to block our progress, and he was able to do so momentarily. But through prayer and the hard work of the judges and the DAs, we incorporated secular mentors into the program, and in doing so we silenced the voice of our adversaries. God's grace prevailed, and we overcame all the obstacles— and the program is in full swing today and thriving!

As you turn the knob to step out of the door, expect some satanic pushback. It's his job; it's what he does. However, don't let him stop you. Move forward expecting God's grace and power to be with you. Possess in your heart the promises of God's strength, victory and wisdom that fill the pages of your Bible. Remember these words of Jesus: "I will build my church, and the gates of Hades will not overcome it" (Matthew 16:18). He didn't say there wouldn't be a fight, but he did say they wouldn't prevail. And don't forget this either: God's power and grace, which thrusts you out the door and sustains you in ministry to your community, is far greater than any resistance that your adversary can muster.

Yes, there are some obstacles for you to overcome in order to cross the threshold and love you community for Christ. However, no matter what the barriers may be, you can break out. John penned these words of Jesus not just for church in Philadelphia but for you as well:

> To the angel of the church in Philadelphia write: These are the words of him who is holy and true, who holds the key of David. What he opens no one can shut, and what he shuts no one can open. I know your deeds. See, I have

placed before you an open door that no one can shut. I know that you have little strength, yet you have kept my word and have not denied my name. (Revelation 3:7-8)

Friend, look: the door for you to engage your community is wide open, courtesy of Jesus himself. Take the bold step and walk through it. You will find someone has been waiting at the threshold for you to walk out.

For Reflection and Discussion

1. What emotions are aroused in your heart as you read Judges 19?

2. Where are places in your community in which you have encountered or seen people with their hands on the threshold?

3. Several barriers that might keep you and your church locked inside were listed in this chapter. What barriers do you find the most difficult to overcome?

4. What fears do you have that impact your community ministry?

5. What's your plan to break out?

6. How will you pray for you and your church to be released into your community?

three

Capturing Passion

Passion is the fuel that burns in the depths of your soul, producing more than just an emotional spark that flickers momentarily and then fizzles out. On the contrary, passion ignites a flame within that burns with permanence. Its heat will inspire you, motivate you and encourage you to pursue what you love while simultaneously empowering you with the strength and tenacity necessary to reach your summit.

You and your church reaching your community is not solely a matter of obligation or duty. It's a matter of passion as well. The mantra is not "Oh, I have to forge a merger with my community because it's what God wants." No, the tone rings more like this: "I get to reach out to my community. I want desperately to engage my community, and I can't wait to get at it!"

We have a duty and an obligation as the church to share Jesus with our community. However, if your service to your community is purely duty-driven, your heart can be absent from the game. Your heart needs to be present. Obligation and duty alone are the equivalent of eating a piece of day-old bread without butter and strawberry jam; they're awful hard to swallow. Passion, on the other hand, adds the sweet honey, the joy of the Lord, to your mission. Not only that but your passion helps direct your efforts and makes love a major motivational factor in all that you do.

Harriet Tubman once said, "Every great dream begins with a dreamer. Always remember, you have within you the strength, the patience and the passion to reach for the stars to change the world." What a powerful quote! She says your passion will help you change your world.

To participate in a divine merger, capturing a passion for your community is premium. Don't think it's not there. You have it—you just have to find it. When you capture your passion, you will be reaching for the stars and changing the lives of people in your community. Capturing your passion may take some work, but it can be done. Here's how.

Be Yourself

One of the temptations we fall into in the church is what I call the cookie-cutter syndrome. It's a form of peer pressure that seeks to conform us not to the image of Jesus but to the image of whatever is hot in our church culture. For example, if you're going to sing, you should sound like so and so. If you're going to have a thriving church, it should look like that church over there. It you reach out to your community, you have to do it exactly like person A or church B.

The problem is that no two people are exactly the same, and no two churches are exactly the same. Each person and each church has a different personality, gift mix, experience and background, and ministry context. Those we try to emulate have a hard enough time just trying to be who they are.

I like to watch old movies on TCM, and I remember one time they were talking about the Rat Pack: Frank Sinatra, Dean Martin, Sammy Davis Jr. and crew. Somehow some young upstart actor had the opportunity to tell Sinatra that he wanted to be just like him. Sinatra's response to the bright-eyed youngster was that he himself had a tough time being Frank Sinatra.

No wonder the Bible tells us not to compare ourselves to each other. It's a vicious trap that robs you of the incredible uniqueness God has fashioned within you. You are one of a kind. There was no one else like you before, and there will be no one else like you when you're long gone. Why destroy the beautiful tapestry woven within your soul by God by trying to be someone or something you are not? Be who God has made you to be—and no one else.

When you embrace who God has made you to be, your new freedom will release a passion in your heart to do God's will. That means your ministry in the community doesn't have to look like anyone else's. Yes, the kingdom goals are the same, but the way you go about accomplishing those goals doesn't have to be the same. You have the freedom to be creative in expressing your ministry as God has placed it in your heart and soul.

I was driving my oldest son, Micah, to school, and we got on the topic of evangelism. I thought this would be a great time to challenge him to reach out to his friends, bring them to church and so on. His response to my sermonette made me think. He said, "Dad, you have your way to reach your friends, and I have my way. We're doing the same thing, but my approach is different from yours." I couldn't say anything; he was right.

Please hear me loud and clear. Be yourself and create your merger in the community the way God shows you. You do not have to be a carbon copy of Joe Success down the road. Your primary objective is to please Jesus Christ. Think about this: Jesus had twelve disciples, none of whom were carbon copies of any other. In their own ways, they all strove to be who Jesus wanted them to be. Being who you are and ministering to your community in a way that is authentic with your makeup will infuse you with passion and joy.

Keep Your Ear to the Ground

Four years ago, Sam Adams, the former mayor of Portland, invited a group of twenty or so people from our community to talk together about the rise of violence in our city. Present that day was a cross-section of individuals including people from the neighborhood, a few pastors, law enforcement officials and the father of a young man who recently had been murdered.

The meeting began with the mayor rattling off a page of statistics that showed the recent upswing of violence in our community. The numbers were alarming and discomforting to say the least. Sitting there, you could hear a collective sigh and see somber faces and heads around the table nodding, as if saying together, "This is a tragedy."

Once the mayor finished sharing the numbers, he started to share his heart. He pleaded with us, saying, "The city is doing all it can to reverse this violent trend, but if there is anything you could do to help, please do it. We need you!" When he finished, the teary-eyed and broken father began to share about his teenage son, whose life had been snuffed out by a stray bullet shot into a group of kids waiting at a bus stop to go home from school. As the father shared his story, the combination of his words and the mayor's plea for help instantly awakened in my heart a passion to engage our church is this community problem.

Sure, I had been aware of the violence prior to the meeting, and I had prayed many times for God to curb the violence in our community. But the passion to engage wasn't present until I heard the hearts of those two men. It wasn't until I heard the community's heart that my passion ignited.

Placing your ear to the ground and listening to what is trans-piring in your community is a way for God to ignite a passion in your heart. An awesome biblical example of the listening-passion equation is found in the life of Nehemiah.

Nehemiah wasn't a pastor or priest; he was a government worker who was in love with God and the city of Jerusalem. Though he loved God and his hometown, the passion to help the people struggling back home became a blaze only after he heard a report from his brother. Prior to hearing of the crisis occurring in his city, he was confined to his job and had no idea God planned to use him to change a community of people. The passion that would move him to action lay dormant within.

Nehemiah 1:1-4 tells us the story of his passion-igniting ex-perience:

> The words of Nehemiah son of Hacaliah: In the month of Kislev in the twentieth year, while I was in the citadel of Susa, Hanani, one of my brothers, came from Judah with some other men, and I questioned them about the Jewish remnant that had survived the exile, and also about Jeru-salem. They said to me, "Those who survived the exile and are back in the province are in great trouble and disgrace. The wall of Jerusalem is broken down, and its gates have been burned with fire." When I heard these things, I sat down and wept. For some days I mourned and fasted and prayed before the God of heaven.

The words that Nehemiah heard that day were flaming coals from heaven. Those few words—"Those who survived the exile and are back in the province are in great trouble and disgrace. The wall of Jerusalem is broken down, and its gates have been burned with fire"—were God's call to him to change his destiny and the misfortune of a community of people who were living in difficult times. The burden God placed within his heart wasn't a shallow emotional experience. It was a transformative force that moved him to risk his own life and comfort for the sake of forging a divine merger with a community in despair. It was a passion that endured through years of difficulty and sacrifice until God's shalom was present in that community.

Listening is easier said than done. Why? You and I live in an extremely loud world where we are relentlessly bombarded by noise. There's our own personal noise, echoing our cares, worries and fears. There's the cultural noise clamoring for our attention, badgering us to align ourselves with the world's priorities and values. There's the noise of the issues and problems negatively affecting our communities. There's the modern-day Goliath on our block, shouting in our ears, "Who do you think you are, little person? I'm here to stay, and there is nothing you or your church can do about it!" Also contributing to the high-decibel assault are the pint-size noisemakers, such as smartphones, computers, televisions and gaming consoles. Don't get me wrong; I enjoy all those, but they are noisy!

I grew up in a family of seven, including my parents. For my mother to have a conversation on the phone in peace and quiet required an act of God. With three boys who thought the entire house was a gym or a baseball diamond, you can imagine the commotion. Her usual words when answering the phone were, "You guys, quiet down in there! How do you expect me to hear with all that noise going on?" My mom's question, or, more accurately, her command, holds true for your ability to hear the voice of God calling you to a place of passion for your community.

I'll put a slight spin on Mom's commentary: "How can you hear the need of your community with all that noise going on?" The answer is that you *can't* hear with all that noise going on. To hear a passion-producing call, you need to create some silence intentionally. Here's how you can push the mute button.

Make the decision to listen. This may seem like a no-brainer, but if you're convinced in your mind there's nothing for you to hear, chances are you won't hear anything. To hear your community calling and God speaking, a personal decision to listen is a must. God has a message he wants to convey to you about your community and your involvement. Make the decision to listen to what God has to say. Some words of Samuel sum it up beautifully: "Speak, for your servant is listening" (1 Samuel 3:10).

Ask for God's help to hear. The ability to hear with your heart a call coming from your community is a gift from God. How many people in your community watch the news, read the papers and search the web to get the latest news about the community? My guess is a lot. Out of the many people who have the daily 411 on the community's woes via the news, the percentage that respond by becoming change-makers is minuscule. People hear information, and it resonates with their heads, not their hearts. They fail to hear a call that stirs a passion to make a difference. Although Nehemiah was a great guy, his ability to hear of the devastation in his hometown and to respond as he did was not because he was such a great guy. He was able to hear because God had a plan and wanted him to be a participant. God graciously gave him the capacity to hear the call and feel the need. His capacity to hear was a gift from God: "Ears that hear and eyes that see—the LORD has made them both" (Proverbs 20:12). God is the one who gives ears to hear; ask him to help you hear the cry of your community.

Ask questions. Nehemiah heard because he asked his brother questions about the city: "I questioned them about the Jewish remnant that survived the exile, and also about Jerusalem" (Nehemiah 1:2). A point of clarification is needed here: he didn't ask questions just to fill his need to talk; he also asked questions so he could *listen.* There's a big difference between the two. Talk with people or visit groups that are knowledgeable about the issue in your community that interests you. Listen prayerfully with open ears and an open heart. God can use your inquiry to communicate to your soul the passion and purpose of his heart.

Put yourself in places to be impacted. If you insulate yourself inside the comfort of your surroundings, hearing the community is going to be very difficult. Listening to your community requires you to take risks and step out into unfamiliar territory. You may have a theory, but you won't really know how people are living, feeling and thinking until you step into their territory. There are a host of doors you can walk through in your community to gain the exposure necessary to hear the voice of God's leading. For instance, you could attend community meetings. Or you discover the concerns of the people outside your church by visiting a school, a homeless shelter, a business luncheon or a low-income apartment complex. Grab a community newspaper; you may find some suggestions there too. Find someone in your church that may have a challenging background, and take him or her out to lunch to hear his or her story. You have tons of options to nestle into that will allow you to hear your community's heart and God's heart. Pick a spot, and go for it!

Welcome a special call of God. There are times when God will supernaturally tell you what you are supposed to do. A great example is found in the apostle Paul's Macedonian call: "During the night Paul had a vision of a man of Macedonia standing and begging him, 'Come over to Macedonia and help us.' After Paul had seen the vision, we got ready at once to leave for Macedonia, concluding that God had called us to preach the gospel to them" (Acts 16:9-10). This passage is used primarily in conjunction with overseas missions, but I believe God gives us a call to our communities as well.

God spoke to Paul in a vision and gave him clear direction. At the time, Macedonia was not on Paul's radar, but it was on God's. The impact of seeing a man standing and begging in the vision produced passion in Paul's heart—to the point that he and his company left at once to preach the gospel in that region. God dealt with Paul in a supernatural way to direct him and impassion him.

There's a beautiful worship song titled "Spirit Breakout." The heart cry of the song is a prayer to God, asking him to manifest his kingdom and glory on earth to heal and mend broken and sinful people. One line in the song asks the question, "Can you hear it, the sound of heaven touching earth?" That's a great question! Can you hear it? Can you hear the sound of heaven touching earth?

Sure you can! Put your ear to the ground, mute the noise and listen to God's voice. Not only can you hear the sound of heaven touching earth, you may see heaven touching earth. You can see the merger because you heard the voice of God and passionately responded in obedience. Your partnership with God is heaven lovingly touching your community.

Your Gift

Passion is the primary DNA strand of a God-given gift. Understand that God not only gives you the ability and graces that are incorporated in the gift, he also lavishly supplies you with the passion to use your gift. Your gifting and passion are a package deal—two peas in a pod!

I think sometimes we are absent-minded when it comes to remembering that dynamic relationship. Many of us have the idea that if we engage our community, we leave our gift in the church to do something in the community that we are un-equipped to do. That alone is a passion killer. God has gifted you, and if those gifts are good enough to use in the four walls of the church, they are good enough to use in your community. There are places in your community where your gifts are needed and will work beautifully.

Betty Dorsey has served Jesus more years than I have been alive. Her commitment to Christ is contagious, and she is pas-sionate about doing his work. She has many talents and gifts, but two of her joys are music and sharing Christ. Since her teenage years, she has played the piano and sung in churches all over the place. Her husband often tells the story of their courtship. He would drive three to four hours from his Air Force base to visit her. If he visited on a Sunday, he had to tag along all day while she played the piano and sang for a number of churches in her hometown. When he tells this story, I never know if he's bragging or lamenting.

I won't get myself in trouble by mentioning Betty's age, but from then until today, the gift is present, and she is still pas-sionate about playing the piano, singing and sharing Jesus. Though she doesn't play nearly as much as she used to in the church, she has found a way to use her gift in our community. Since 2006, Betty and a few other women from our church conduct a worship service at an assisted living facility. Every Friday, the residents there gather for a time of biblical teaching, singing, prayer and conversation. Since many of the people don't have the ability to come and go at will, and some seldom have visitors, the service is the highlight of their week. This Christmas, the team received a beautiful card from the management, thanking them and expressing how much the residents look forward to their coming every Friday.

When you talk to Betty about playing, singing and sharing Jesus at the facility every Friday, don't expect to get some old, worn-out, woe-is-me response. On the contrary, she is pumped about how God is using her and the team in their ministry to our community. She told me once, "Oh, Pastor Mark, this is a wonderful ministry!"

I agree with her; it is a wonderful ministry—and Carol Lee would agree too. In December of 2014, Betty and her group had concluded their service and had finished talking and praying with people when she noticed Carol Lee sitting in her wheel-chair. She wasn't going back to her room as usual but simply sat there, not moving. Betty went over and started a conversation with her. Leaning forward and whispering to Betty, Carol Lee confided, "I don't believe I know God." Over the next several minutes, Betty shared Scripture with her and led her to faith in Jesus. They prayed together, and Carol left the service with joy and peace in her heart.

The following week, Betty returned eagerly to see Carol Lee. But a few days after she came to faith in Christ, Carol Lee had an appointment to keep—an appointment in heaven with Jesus. Though Betty said it was hard to see her new friend go, she re-joiced because Carol Lee made it in the door and did not die on the threshold.

Betty's story is a great example of how a God-given gift can generate a passion for your community. As Paul told Timothy, his son in the ministry, "For this reason I remind you to fan into flame the gift of God, which is in you through the laying on of my hands" (2 Timothy 1:6). You have a gift given to you by God. Fan it into flame by finding a place where you can use it in your community. You'll discover that having a passion in your heart for your community will not be a problem.

When Love Is Lost in Zeal

In some parts of the church, there has been a wonderful resurgence in a focus on social justice. Critical conversations regarding issues affecting the poor and fatherlessness, race and biblical responsibility are being hashed out at the table. Thousands across our country are realizing for the first time the importance of tackling the tough issues that exist in cities and communities across our nation. I raise my voice with many others in gratitude to God for this movement and shout, "Hallelujah!"

However, in our zeal for social justice, it's critical for us to understand that we attack these issues not because we are lovers of the issues themselves, but because, at our core, we are lovers of God and people. I can confess to you from my own personal experience that it is very easy to become engrossed in the issue and lose sight of the people.

Paul says it best in the "Love Chapter," unequivocally telling you and me that everything we do—from speaking to administering social justice—is worthless if love for people is absent from our hearts.

> If I speak in the tongues of men and of angels, but have not love, I am only a resounding gong or a clanging cymbal. If I have the gift of prophecy and can fathom all mysteries and all knowledge, and if I have a faith that can move

mountains, but have not love, I am nothing. If I give all I possess to the poor and surrender my body to the flames, but have not love, I gain nothing.

Love is patient, love is kind. It does not envy, it does not boast, it is not proud. It is not rude, it is not self-seeking, it is not easily angered, it keeps no record of wrongs. Love does not delight in evil but rejoices with the truth. It always protects, always trusts, always hopes, always perseveres. Love never fails. But where there are prophecies, they will cease; where there are tongues, they will be stilled; where there is knowledge, it will pass away. For we know in part and we prophesy in part, but when perfection comes, the imperfect disappears.

When I was a child, I talked like a child, I thought like a child, I reasoned like a child. When I became a man, I put childish ways behind me. Now we see but a poor reflection as in a mirror; then we shall see face to face. Now I know in part; then I shall know fully, even as I am fully known. And now these three remain: faith, hope and love. But the greatest of these is love. (1 Corinthians 13)

Much could be said about this passage, and truthfully, it is why I'm writing this book. Where love is present, you can't help but be passionate about helping others. Love is active and progressive—it will not allow you to sit by idly and navel-gaze. John 3:16 tells us that God loved the world so much that he acted. He gave his only son to us so that if we believe in him, we will live. When you love your community, your passion will erupt into redeeming action. You won't be able to contain it; you'll just have to let redeeming lava flow throughout the streets where you live.

When Jesus endured his Passion, he expressed the passionate love he had for the people of Jerusalem, loudly lamented with tears, "Jerusalem, Jerusalem, you who kill the prophets and stone those sent to you, how often I have longed to gather your children together, as a hen gathers her chicks under her wings, but you were not willing" (Matthew 23:37). Ironically, even though Jesus had experienced repeated rejections in that city, his love and passion for its people were still present—to the point of causing him to weep.

Anthony Jordan is passionate for the youth in our community. If you talk to Anthony for longer than five minutes about kids who are particularly far outside the walls of the church, he is likely to shed a tear or two. Anthony grew up in a single-parent household; his dad abandoned the family when he was two years old. As he grew older, Anthony's anger and antisocial behavior grew as well. It wasn't until his sophomore year in high school that someone was able to get his attention—a coach. Coach McPherson told him that if he continued on the path he was on, he would end up in jail, dead or on the street corner, begging. What impacted Anthony was not only the words Coach McPherson spoke but also his actions. According to Anthony, the coach not only talked the talk, but he got in the dirt with him and helped him change his way of life.

Out of the bumps and bruises Anthony suffered as a youth, God forged a deep love and passion for the youth who are "the least of these" in our community (see Mathew 25:40, 45). For the last twenty years, Anthony has coached three thousand kids in our community. He has instructed them not only on how to play a sport but also on how to grow up and be good men who raise good families and contribute to the well-being of their community.

Anthony is also the cofounder and president of the Portland Leadership Foundation (PLF), whose mission is to strengthen and develop leadership for the spiritual and social renewal of Portland. In the last eight years, PLF has been responsible for providing 183 full-ride scholarships to students that otherwise wouldn't have been able to afford a college education.

Portland Leadership Foundation was also instrumental in helping launch Embrace Oregon, an initiative in which seventy-eight churches participate in making care boxes for kids who are in the foster care system, providing respite for foster care providers and encouraging churchgoers to adopt foster kids. The goal is to connect caring people with vulnerable children through partnership with the Department of Human Services as well as local Child Welfare offices for the thriving of our communities. What's happening with Embrace Oregon is absolutely phenomenal.

Key to Anthony's involvement is that he doesn't simply feel that the issues are important—though they certainly are. His passion to make a difference is fueled by the love God has placed in his heart for kids.

My prayer is that, like Nehemiah, Betty and Anthony, you will capture a passion for your community. Listen to the voice of the Lord, fan into flame your God-given gift, and love the people where you life. If you do, your passion will ignite and carry you into the highways and byways of your community with joy.

For Reflection and Discussion

1. What is the driving passion in your life?

2. Have you ever felt the pressure to be and do something that's not you? Explain.

3. How do you think your passion can translate into community ministry?

4. What are the gifts that God has given you? How could you use them in your community?

5. Do you find it is easy or difficult to love your community? Why?

6. How will you pray for the igniting of your passion and your church's passion for your community?

four

Presenting an Authentic Jesus

It was a typical hot afternoon in the city of Jerusalem. The streets were buzzing with people going about their business as usual. As it was close to the hour of prayer, people were making their way up to the temple to pray. Included in the crowd were three people with two very different agendas. Peter and John went with the primary goal of praying and seeking the face of God. The third man was a full-time beggar. Due to his disability, friends carried him daily to the temple so that he could beg for money in order to survive. His station was right in front of the gate called Beautiful, and he sat there day after day and year after year, broken and begging.

The gate was an impressive structure. Sixty feet wide and seventy-five feet high, it required at least twenty men to operate it. Besides the massive size, the structure was made of the finest Corinthian brass and was overlaid with intricate ornamentation. Its brilliance made it one of the most well-known and expensive pieces of the city's landscape—so much so that the people called it "Beautiful" (Acts 3:2, 10).

There is something wrong with this picture. Here you have a piece of architecture so impressive that it stuns your senses, and you also have a man made in the image of God with dignity and honor, a person whose intrinsic value far exceeds the worth of a million beautiful gates, begging for his survival in a place. His plea for life is not a one-time occurrence but a daily occupation, so much so that his cry for alms is known throughout his community. Yet through all the years of his begging, who ever offered to give him an occupation that would foster self-worth and dignity?

While the dazzle of the gate's brass and the glitter of the ornamentation sparkle in the sunlight, there lies a broken man who is a part of the community. If we look really hard, we see that the sun is not only reflecting the gate's beauty but also illuminating the brokenness of a man and a community need. A contradictory picture—a wrong picture!

But there is something right with this picture too.

Enter Peter and John. While they are on their way to the temple, they see and hear the man begging. Knowing the man's need and the value of the gate, Peter responded, "Silver or gold I do not have"(Acts 3:6). In other words, they were not going to address the surface needs of the begging man by giving him gold or silver. They understood that to address the core source of his brokenness an authentic presentation of Jesus was needed. Hence, "Silver or gold I do not have, but . . . in the name of Jesus Christ of Nazareth, walk" (Acts 3:6). They took the man by the hand, giving him a tangible touch, and by the proclamation of the name of Jesus, a miracle happened. The crippled man's life and dignity were restored. His life became beautiful, and he and the community felt the life-giving impact of Jesus Christ.

In our communities, many discrepancies exist between the beauty and the brokenness. I was preaching once in South Africa, and we went to visit a site that the church had adopted in order to make the living conditions better and to share the authentic Jesus. For many years, this community of people had no running water in a city where having adequate plumbing was not an insurmountable task.

The layers of garbage and debris on their land made it resemble an excavation site. They walked on, slept on and lived on garbage that was at least eight feet deep. The children had no schooling. Some people lived in makeshift huts, and others lived on any cardboard they could find. The situation was so dire that we wept as we shared God's love with this severely disenfranchised community. The whole community was crippled and begging. Sadly, directly across the street was one of the largest big-name car dealerships in the world. What a paradox!

Like Peter and John, the church there decided to reach out its hand to help a broken community experience beauty through an authentic representation of Jesus Christ.

Despite the trophies in our churches and communities, there are broken people all around us, people whose lives are in chaos, darkness and pain. To minister to these people, we have to engage our communities. They are outside the doors of our churches. They are across the street or across town. They are our neighbors. Like Peter and John, our responsibility is to give them Jesus, a Jesus who is present in word and deed, right where they are.

The Jesus John Knew

John the Baptist had the greatest prophetic assignment in the Scriptures. His job was to prepare the way for Jesus. He had the unique privilege of recognizing Jesus through the revelation of the Father and the task of revealing him to Israel.

> The next day John saw Jesus coming toward him and said, "Look, the Lamb of God, who takes away the sin of the world! This is the one I meant when I said, 'A man who

comes after me has surpassed me because he was before me.' I myself did not know him, but the reason I came baptizing with water was that he might be revealed to Israel."

Then John gave this testimony: "I saw the Spirit come down from heaven as a dove and remain on him. I would not have known him, except that the one who sent me to baptize with water told me, 'The man on whom you see the Spirit come down and remain is the one who will baptize with the Holy Spirit.' I have seen and I testify that this is the Son of God." (John 1:29-34)

John says that the purpose of his baptismal ministry was to reveal Jesus to Israel. He also makes it clear that his ability to reveal Jesus depended on the Father showing him who Jesus was. God made Jesus unmistakably identifiable to John. There was no guesswork involved. First, God spoke to John and told him the man upon whom he would see the Spirit come down and rest would be the Son of God. Second, John actually witnessed the fulfillment of what was told to him. With his own eyes, he saw the Holy Spirit descend in the form of a dove and rest upon Jesus. Hearing and seeing what God had spoken to him caused John to give a credible testimony of Jesus' authenticity as the Son of God.

As the end of his life approached, John was no longer sure about the things he had once believed. Like us all from time to time, the bedrock of his faith was cracking under the weight of difficulty. In a state of crisis, John sent his disciples to Jesus to ask the question, "Are you the one who is to come, or should we expect someone else?" (Matthew 11:3). Jesus' response brought John reassurance of who he is.

When John heard in prison what Christ was doing, he sent his disciples to ask him, "Are you the one who was to come, or should we expect someone else?"

Jesus replied, "Go back and report to John what you hear and see: The blind receive sight, the lame walk, those who have leprosy are cured, the deaf hear, the dead are raised, and the good news is preached to the poor. Blessed is the man who does not fall away on account of me." (Matthew 11:2-6)

Jesus authenticates that he is indeed the one to come by validating his person via his mission and ministry exploits:

The blind see.

The lame walk.

The lepers are healed.

The gospel is preached to the poor.

Something to consider is that Jesus could have authenticated himself to John in a plethora of ways. He could have spoken of mysteries concerning God or heaven that humanity had never heard before. He could have arranged for John to experience a theophany or for an angelic visitation to occur, but he did not. Jesus chose to authenticate his person to John by describing the execution of mission and ministry and by encouraging John not to fall away.

Hearing of Jesus' ministry was all that was necessary for John to patch the cracks of his battered faith. The admonition to endure was adequate to bring John back to his original testimony that Jesus was the One.

Like John, our church communities are in crisis mode. All of the physical, social, economic and spiritual needs have placed our communities in a tailspin of confusion and doubt about who Jesus really is. Unlike John, many in our community have never witnessed or experienced the authentic Jesus. Instead of going to Jesus in search of reassurance, our communities are moving in rapid speed in search of another. What they are finding is a less-than-adequate knockoff rather than the one who genuinely loves them and can help them—Jesus of Nazareth.

Jesus' interaction with John raises an essential question for ministering to our communities: How is the church to represent or present Jesus authentically in our communities? Upon closer examination, the path toward answering that question is given partly in Jesus' response to John. Jesus communicates four essential missional truths that authenticate his person: missional priorities, missional proclamation, missional presence and missional perseverance.

Missional Priorities

Incorporated in Jesus' mission was the priority to help broken and disenfranchised people. He told John that the blind see, the lame walk, the lepers are healed, the deaf hear and the dead are raised. All of these acts of mercy and miracles have to do with improving the quality of life and alleviating human suffering in the here and now. One of my favorite passages related to this is in Isaiah 61:

> The Spirit of the Sovereign LORD is on me,
>   because the LORD has anointed me
>   to preach good news to the poor.
> He has sent me to bind up the brokenhearted,
>   to proclaim freedom for the captives
>   and release from darkness for the prisoners,

to proclaim the year of the LORD's favor
 and the day of vengeance of our God,
to comfort all who mourn,
 and provide for those who grieve in Zion—
to bestow on them a crown of beauty instead of ashes,
the oil of gladness instead of mourning,
and a garment of praise instead of a spirit of despair.
They will be called oaks of righteousness,
 a planting of the LORD for the display of his splendor.
They will rebuild the ancient ruins
 and restore the places long devastated;
they will renew the ruined cities
 that have been devastated for generations. (Isaiah 61:1-4)

Speaking of Jesus, these verses tell us he was empowered by the Holy Spirit, anointed by God to help hurting people. Aspects of his mission included

- binding up the brokenhearted

- proclaiming freedom for the captives

- releasing the prisoners from their dark dungeons

- comforting and providing for those in distress and pain

- transforming and empowering lives into something beautiful and fruitful

In our communities, we have brokenhearted people everywhere, from the single mother who is struggling to feed her kids to the homeless person who believes his doom is sealed. We have prisoners locked up in our penal institutions and prisoners that daily walk the streets, crying inwardly for deliverance. In our communities are those who swim daily in the waters of pain, slowly losing hope of ever making it to shore. Yes, there are beautiful aspects of our communities, but we cannot allow the glitz of the brass to blind us to the needs of the hurting. Jesus isn't blind to the pain in our communities, and the church can't be either. Jesus' missional priority was to extend help to hurting people then, and it is his priority now.

At Life Change, one of the ways we equip people for ministry to hurting people is through our School of Ministry. It's a one-year program that focuses on character and service. We have a segment where students write out the main points of their life story in two or three pages. The goal of the lesson is to equip them to share their story of transformation effectively with others.

One night, Anthony told his story. It was riveting. He told the class of forty or so that between ages five and seven he was confined to the house due to a very bad case of asthma. The inability to hang out with his brothers and play with the other kids was a real bummer. When he turned eight, one of his brother's friends began molesting him. Not only was he violated sexually, but his abuser also threatened and beat him, placing him in a prison of fear and telling him that if he told anyone, the same thing would happen to his brothers. The abuse and molestation threw him into a state of confusion and an identity crisis that he wrestled with far into his adult life.

School was also a challenge for Anthony. His inability to learn like other kids due to a learning disability produced more shame. On top of his inner turmoil, his brothers and friends rubbed salt in the wound by making his disability the butt of their jokes and entertainment. When he turned twelve, he discovered that he was a good singer and artist. These newfound talents provided him some comfort and social validation. However, the inner load he carried was too much for him to overcome. By age fourteen, Anthony began casually experimenting with drugs.

After his teen years, he married and had two children. Eight years later, he left his wife and children and began a twenty-seven-year drug binge. He was on a hellish merry-go-round and could not get off. Anthony describes it as a time of wild women, pleasure and addiction. During this period, he married again, only to have his wife die suddenly. He told the class that he didn't treat this wife right either, but she still loved him. His life was beyond a mess.

On November 7, 2007, Anthony cried out to Jesus from the garage he was living in. A godly Christian mother had raised and prayed for him, but the pain had been so deep, none of that had made any sense to him. He said, "For twenty-seven years, I'd been trapped in a prison with no gate out. . . . In the turmoil of my pain, I cried out to Jesus. I said, 'Jesus, if you are real like my mother says, and if you can do what she says you can do, then make yourself real to me and help me!'"

He went on to tell the class that while he was praying, it was like a Damascus Road experience. For the first time in over forty years, his chains fell off, the prison gate opened, and he walked out, never to go back. Needless to say, people in the class were wiping away tears and praising Jesus for his goodness. Jesus, whose missional priority was to help broken and hurting people, had touched Anthony.

Luke 4:16-20 places Isaiah 61 in the mosaic of Jesus' earthly ministry:

> He went to Nazareth, where he had been brought up, and on the Sabbath day he went into the synagogue, as was his custom. And he stood up to read. The scroll of the prophet

Isaiah was handed to him. Unrolling it, he found the place where it is written: "The Spirit of the Lord is on me, because he has anointed me to preach good news to the poor. He has sent me to proclaim freedom for the prisoners and recovery of sight for the blind, to release the oppressed, to proclaim the year of the Lord's favor."

Then he rolled up the scroll, gave it back to the attendant and sat down. The eyes of everyone in the synagogue were fastened on him. (Luke 4:16-20)

Jesus concludes the reading of Isaiah 61 by telling his listeners, "Today this scripture is fulfilled in your hearing" (Luke 4:21). Today hurting and broken people in our communities desperately need a touch from Jesus. Your church can give that touch. It can present to the community an authentic Jesus by making the needs of the people a missional priority. As the late Dr. Joe Aldrich used to say, you can't preach to someone unless they know that you love them.

Missional Proclamation

In the middle of a discussion on counseling during my seminary days, my theology professor made a statement I will never forget. If my recollection serves me right, we were talking about the 1980s trend of being a counselor in the pulpit rather than a proclaimer of Scripture. My professor said, "I am convinced that we can indeed make people better sinners, but is that all we are called to do?" I have never forgotten those words. And I have been in many situations where it would have been easier to leave the proclamation of the gospel out of a situation than to include it.

As is apparent in Jesus' words from Luke 4, proclaiming the good news was an integral part of his mission. He was anointed to preach good news to the poor. He was called to proclaim the year of the Lord's favor. Proclaiming the good news was central to Jesus' mission, and he did it.

Solomon personifies wisdom as a female preacher whose voice is heard crying out to people in all the community gathering places of the city:

> Lady Wisdom goes out in the street and shouts.
> At the town center she makes her speech.
> In the middle of the traffic she takes her stand.
> At the busiest corner she calls out. (Proverbs 1:20-21
> *The Message*)

The church is the voice of lady wisdom today in the streets, in the town center, in the middle of the traffic and on the busiest corners. Today the church is the voice of wisdom proclaiming the gospel of Jesus Christ in all segments of her community.

If I can be bold, I believe it is ludicrous to engage our communities with only good works and no proclamation of the gospel. We are the church; we are not simply a philanthropic agency or organization to better humanity, as great and needed as those are. We are God's community. We have a redemptive message that addresses need on more than a social, physical or economic level.

Our message speaks to the core of humanity's deepest and sometimes most neglected need: redemption and peace with God. I'm not saying that every time we hand out a piece of bread to a hungry soul we need to make sure we familiarize them with the Four Spiritual Laws or some other evangelistic tool. But just as we have a strategy to engage our community in good works, we also need a strategy for proclaiming the gospel. When Jesus sent out the seventy-two disciples to the various towns, he told them to heal the sick and proclaim the kingdom (Luke 10:9). Their mission was not just about giving physical or social aid; it was a synthesis of doing good deeds and proclaiming the message.

In the book *Churches That Make a Difference*, the authors write,

> The twentieth century saw a divisive argument between social gospel churches that focused one-sidedly on social action, and evangelistic churches that insisted that leading people to Christ was the only truly important mission of the church. The tragic results of that long argument have not entirely disappeared, but we have made great progress. Evangelical leaders today widely agree that biblical churches must combine word and deed, doing both evangelism and social ministry.[1]

We live in a culture where it seems every ideology, dogma or religion is in vogue except the gospel. The challenge many churches face today is overcoming the antagonism in their communities regarding the gospel. Granted, we could mull over this point, exploring the reasons why the antagonism exists, ranging from church failings—both historical and present—to abuses to shifts in culture. But whatever the reason or reasons, they must be overcome, and the gospel must be preached.

Alternatively, to put it in postmodern vernacular, the story must be told. Our churches need eagerness and God-given confidence to share the gospel effectively in their communities. Each community of faith should embrace Paul's passion for sharing the gospel:

> That is why I am so eager to preach the gospel also to you who are at Rome. I am not ashamed of the gospel, because

it is the power of God for the salvation of everyone who believes: first for the Jew, then for the Gentile. For in the gospel the righteousness from God is revealed, a right-eousness that is by faith from first to last, just as it is written: "The righteous will live by faith." (Romans 1:15-17)

Our churches should tell the story of God's love for humanity, how he sent Jesus Christ to die for the entire human race, how through his death on the cross and his resurrection from the dead we can place our faith in him, and how through repentance and trust we can experience eternal life and an intimate rela-tionship with God (John 3:16). If we are mute regarding the gospel, we give people physical bread to eat but leave them to hunger again. By sharing the gospel, we give them the oppor-tunity to receive Jesus Christ, the Bread of Life, which will keep them from ever hungering again. Our communities are waiting to hear the gospel, and the church has the responsibility and privilege of proclaiming the message.

Power House Temple. Pastor Mary Overstreet Smith is a re-markable leader. The name of her church speaks for itself: Power House. Her church does not sprawl over acres, nor do thousands attend her services, but the work she and the church do in their community is mega in the truest expression of the word. Hon-estly, how God has and is using this church, which might be considered small by the standards of many, is nothing short of miraculous.

In 2005, when Hurricane Katrina struck, Pastor Smith was watching the news and felt in her heart that she needed to do something. At the time she had only $850 in the bank. Prompted by the Lord, she called her realtor and asked him to put her house on the market. In a matter of twenty-three hours and fifteen minutes, the house sold. Adding to the miracle, the money was in her account within a couple of days. She then rented a number of vans, moved forty families from New Orleans to Oregon and secured twenty-six apartments for them. The church provided shelter, food and clothing for the families.

Pastor Smith soon discovered that many of these families had no medical care. This led her to collaborate with a doctor to start a free medical clinic just feet away from her church for people who could not afford health care. The clinic now has more than thirty volunteer doctors and nurses on its roster. Hundreds in the community regularly receive care that would not have been provided if Pastor Smith had stayed inside the walls of her church. The health clinic is not the only area where Power House reaches into the community. They also have a transitional home for men and a center for autistic children as well as other services.

For over fifteen years, Pastor Smith has looked after her great-grandson Sir Millage. Early one morning in 2006, Sir was meandering down the Broadway Bridge when police officers approached him and asked what he was doing. Sir, who is autistic and functions on the level of a two-year-old, was unable to respond properly. When the officers saw that Sir was not complying with any of their motions or commands, they shot him with Tasers multiple times.

In response to the situation, a vigil was held where the community and clergy gathered to speak out against the injustice done to Sir. During the vigil, a clear call was given for the community to take a stand to end injustices inflicted on the vulnerable in our community. A bold call was given for the city of Portland to be a place where the government and police protect those who suffer from mental disabilities.

As one of the speakers said, "Today is a day where we lift our voices so that our cry may be heard in our city that this type of brutality must stop!" Their voices were heard, and the vigil furthered the conversation in the city concerning protection for the mentally disabled. In conducting a vigil to confront the injustice, Pastor Smith reached beyond her own pain into her community.

Pastor Smith's heart went out to the parents in the community who lovingly spend twenty-four hours a day caring for their autistic children. To meet that community need, she started the Sir J. Millage Drop-Off Center, where parents and caregivers can drop off people with autism for a few hours while they take a break or take care of other responsibilities. The center is equipped with games and computers and has safe rooms where the visitors cannot hurt themselves. There is no fee charged for the service, and those that utilize the center greatly appreciate that. The SJM Drop-Off Center is a unique merger where Jesus is colliding with a segment of the community he dearly loves.

With all the community work Power House is doing, one thing is for sure: The message of Jesus Christ is proclaimed. Pastor Smith says, "Providing the help that people really need opens their hearts up to you. When people you are serving are drawn to you, you must genuinely listen to them and to God." She says it is essential to hear the heart of men and women and to listen to the voice of God. She states that it's in those moments you have the chance to share the Word and take advantage of the opportunity to proclaim Christ.

Adams Elementary School. Churches also have a call to proclaim God's righteousness and justice to inequities in their communities. My friend Bishop Kenny Martin pastored a small inner-city church in St. Louis. Across the street was a dilapidated elementary school that was scheduled to be demolished.

The only activity occurring at Adams Elementary at the time was open-gym days operated by Pastor Kenny and the church. There was still a flicker of hope in the community that the school could be restored to its former glory. But, according to Pastor Kenny, the superintendent told him at one point, "This school is going to be torn down."

Shortly after that discussion, a neighborhood meeting was held, and a developer came to present his plan for a new development on the school site. Feeling the unease in the room, Pastor Kenny rose and said, "You can't come and strip our community of its value." After the meeting, Pastor Kenny organized marches with the slogan "Save our school!" Everyone showed up: young and the old, black and white, Protestant and Catholic and otherwise. The response was overwhelming.

Today the school is still there, but it is now a state-of-the-art elementary school. The city and donors have poured millions into the school, but it was the prophetic proclamation of the church that started the process. That prophetic voice kept the old school in place so that it could be remodeled. God gives the church a voice to speak prophetically and proclaim his justice and righteousness to issues in our communities.

Missional Presence

Sometimes I believe my kids think my childhood was back during early American history. Whenever they want to inquire about my life before their birth, the question starts with something like, "Dad, back in the olden days, did you . . . ?"

Well! Back in the "olden days" when we were kids, we used to congregate in Miss Tolan's front yard. On those hot summer days, we would play and tell slightly inflated stories. Part of the entertainment was the debate that occurred after the story ended. You could hear a crescendo of voices aimed at the story-teller, with shouts of "No way! That didn't really happen! You're lying!" to which the storyteller would respond by spending the next hour defending the authenticity of his tale.

During those olden days, we always had background music, courtesy of our handheld AM transistor radio. One of our favorite songs back then was the James Taylor classic, "You've Got a Friend." No matter where we were in our discussion, when that song came across the airwaves, we transitioned from tall-tale critics to a community choir. Everybody knew all the words, so grabbing a comb or a stick, or just clenching a fist, we had our makeshift microphones in hand. Together we sang,

> You just call out my name, and you know where ever I am
> I'll come running to see you again.
> Winter, spring, summer, or fall, all you have to do is call
> and I'll be there, yeah, yeah, you've got a friend.

Missional presence is being there—being present and being a friend. Father absenteeism highlights the need for presence well. The absence of a father has the potential to create a myriad of issues for a child. Just as a child needs a mother present, that child needs a father present. Studies show that children who have no father present are more likely to experience poverty, teenage pregnancy, imprisonment and many other social and interpersonal problems. Through relationships, we give and receive love to and from one another. Through relationships, we learn about others and ourselves. Through relationships, we grow and mature. And through relationships, we model Christ and share him with the world.

All relationships create complex issues. Our marriages and families have their own sets of relational challenges. Our churches can be occupied with chronic relational problems that are as much a part of our congregations as our church councils and stained-glass windows. Moreover, the community is filled with racial, economic, moral and other issues that make relationship formation difficult and slow.

However, let's put relational dynamics and complexities aside for the moment and look at the obvious: A relationship cannot exist without presence. For a husband to have a relationship with his wife, both must be present. For a father to have a relationship with his children, he must be there. For a church to have relationship with people in need in their community, it must be *in* the community. Jesus' response to John in Matthew 11:2-6 reveals that for Jesus to preach the good news and to heal and bless people, he had to be present with them. He had to go to them where they were before they came to where he was. Hence, missional presence, incarnational ministry.

Being There

The life of Jesus was about being present. He was God incarnate. He was the Word made flesh that lived with us. He was God living in a human body, come to the broken community of our world, a place filled with languishing humanity—the blind, hungry, thirsty, lost and dying. He came to us—a people powerless to help themselves—and made himself accessible. He put himself within an arm's reach of our pitiful grasp and then reached out not only to hold our hands but also to embrace our very souls. His embrace changed our story from one of death and dying to one of joy, faith and hope.

I'm so glad he came and was and is present! To be present means you go where the people are, not expecting them to come to you. Missional presence is being there, but in order to be there, you have to go there.

Too many times in our churches we expect people in need to come to us instead of us going to them. But missional presence is proactive; we go where the needs are, just as Jesus did. We do not wait for them to come to us. We are to follow Jesus' example, as the apostle Peter said:

> You know what has happened throughout Judea, beginning in Galilee after the baptism that John preached—how God anointed Jesus of Nazareth with the Holy Spirit and power, and how he went around doing good and healing all who were under the power of the devil, because God was with him. (Acts 10:37-38)

Jesus went to places in his ministry community and dealt with needs and issues that we face in our communities today. For example, he went

- to Samaria and dealt with gender and race issues with the woman at the well (John 4);
- to Bethany to have dinner in the house of Simon the Leper, whose very name suggests a negative social stigma (Mark 14);
- to a funeral in a town, where he addressed the grief of a mother whose son had died (Luke 7);
- to bat for the children who were in need of safety and his blessing (Matthew 19:13-15);
- to make sure his mother was taken care of (John 19:26-27); and
- to the cross to give us everything that we need for our life and relationship with God and others for eternity.

And the list of goes on.

To be missionally present, like Jesus, we need to go to the place or places in our community that God puts on our hearts. In the words of Frederick Buechner, "The place God calls you to is the place where your deep gladness and the world's deep hunger meet."[2] Presenting an authentic Jesus in our community requires us to be present at the place of need to which God directs us. A line of our missional song to our community should be, "I will be there; yes, I will. You've got a friend."

Included in Jesus' consolation to John were the words, "Blessed is he who does not fall away because of Me" (Matthew 11:6 MEV). Jesus' word addresses the temptation we all face at times to give up under the cost of serving him. It is not always easy! In essence, Jesus tells John to hang in there and not quit.

There's an old saying in the African American church: "I'm gonna hang in there and see what the end is gonna be!" When it comes to ministering an authentic Jesus to our communities, perseverance is a premium. We have to set our sights on the finish line and not get derailed by the rough terrain or the long bends in the road. We have to possess an internal determination to hang in there and see what the end is going to be. It's like the young employee who asked the senior employee, "How did you manage to work so long in the factory?" He replied, "I just got up and went to work every day." Perseverance!

Missional Perseverance

On the corner of Martin Luther King Boulevard and Shaver every weekend and some weekdays, we used to hear the voice of someone crying into a bullhorn, "Jesus loves you, and he can change your life." That voice belonged to Rev. Chester Staples, an old-fashioned, gospel-preaching, singing evangelist. His passion was to share the message of Jesus Christ with his community. Many years, without fail, he would step onto his street-corner pulpit and sing and preach to those passing by on foot or on bikes, in cars or in buses, and even flying overhead. Everybody in the community knew that, rain or shine, Rev. Staples would be at his post.

He had plenty of mockers and haters, but he made his way into the heart of the community. I remember my grandmother speaking fondly of him and saying "amen" as his words reverberated from the bullhorn around the corner. Many others echoed her sentiment. My wife, who lived across town as a girl, said her mother had great respect for Rev. Staples, even though she was not a Christ-follower at the time.

As I reflected on Rev. Staples, I asked myself the question, *How could a person engaged in a ministry that is a bit unorthodox and slightly annoying touch the heart of a community?* Think about it. A bullhorn? Really? I have seen and heard some street preachers that have gotten on my nerves—and I love preaching.

But Rev. Staples penetrated the heart of a community with the love of Jesus Christ, not by his eloquence but by his perseverance. He was faithful to what Jesus had called him to do— not for a few months but for many years. Over time he broke through the ridicule and mockery, and people saw a faithful man who loved them and showed them Jesus. He didn't get paid for what he did, nor did he have multitudes flocking around him. However, day by day, month by month and year by year, he persevered, and a community saw Jesus by watching and listening to a man with a bullhorn on the corner of Martin Luther King and Shaver.

For the church to show Jesus to our community, we can't give up. We have to persevere. It takes a while for some people to get it. If we quit too soon, we miss out on the wonderful revelation of Jesus that God wants to give our communities.

The picture of Jesus that God is creating for our communities is not a snapshot taken on your iPhone. God is creating a masterpiece that takes time to unfold. Therefore, we can't quit until God says stop.

The words of this poem by an unknown author give us some good advice regarding perseverance:

> When things go wrong, as they sometimes will,
> When the road you're trudging seems all uphill,
> When the funds are low and the debts are high,
> And you want to smile, but you have to sigh,
> When care is pressing you down a bit,
> Rest, if you must, but don't you quit.
> Life is queer with its twists and turns,
> As every one of us sometimes learns,
> And many a failure turns about
> When he might have won had he stuck it out.
> Don't give up though the pace seems slow.
> You may succeed with another blow.
> Often the goal is nearer than
> It seems to a faint and faltering man.
> Often the struggler has given up
> When he might have captured the victor's cup.
> And he learned too late when the night slipped down
> How close he was to the golden crown.
> Success is failure turned inside out—
> The silver tint of the clouds of doubt.
> And you never can tell how close you are;
> It may be near when it seems so far.

So stick to the fight when you're hardest hit—
It's when things seem worst that you must not quit.

Church, your community needs to see Jesus. Don't quit. Persevere.

Summing Up

The intent of God is that we present an authentic Jesus to our broken communities. Like Peter and John ministering to the disabled man at the gate called Beautiful, the church has the opportunity to collaborate with God and see the needy areas of our communities move from brokenness to beauty. If we are going to affect the crippled areas of our communities, we must have a missional priority, proclamation, presence and perseverance. Then we can extend our hands to the areas of our assigned ministry. We can boldly declare, "In Jesus' name, rise up and walk." We will have the joy of seeing broken people walking and leaping and praising God because they have encountered the authentic Jesus.

For Reflection and Discussion

1. In your own words, why do you believe it's important for your community to see an authentic representation of Jesus Christ?

2. What are some of the conflicting images of Jesus you see being presented in your community?

3. Describe the climate of your community in terms of its openness to hearing the message of the gospel.

4. What are some ways you can present an authentic Jesus to your community through your life and ministry?

5. Perseverance is key to allowing Jesus to be seen in your community. What are some challenges that tempt you to quit too soon, and how do you combat them?

6. What are ways you can pray for yourself and your church as you consider presenting an authentic Jesus to your community?

five

Community Navigation

Ever had a casual conversation in which someone unknowingly made a statement that transformed the way you
think? This happened to me one day after a Hebrew class in
seminary.

Class had just wrapped up, and Dr. Colsen and I ended up
walking out of the classroom together. Stepping outside into
a rare Portland sunny day, we started to chat about ministry
and culture. We eventually landed on the topic of stereotypes
and discussed our propensity to attempt to squeeze everyone and
everything into one big shoe. Dr. Colsen's perspective-
changing comment to me on that issue was, "No group of
people is monolithic."

You might say, "Yeah, Mark, that's a no-brainer. Everybody is
not the same. I get that." But I contend that while most of us
know this to be true intuitively, sometimes our actions say
otherwise. When individuals and churches talk about reaching
their community, they are often quick to say that a certain
method worked somewhere else, so it should work in their situation as well. Wouldn't it be nice if it were that simple?

Just like all people in a particular race are not all the same, no
community is like any other. Our communities are incredibly

diverse in terms of people, problems and politics. Ministry to your community is not a one-shoe-fits-all scenario.

That being said, it's pretty clear that for us to reach our communities we need more than one shoe. By no means does this mean that you or I or even your church is required to be everything to everyone in your community. However, it does mean that God's assignment for you in your community is vital. Herein lies the challenge: God may be calling you to collide with a segment of your community that is different from you. The people you are called to serve may differ in their economic standing, values, ethnicity or location. In light of the differences, your response to God may be, "Lord, are you sure? I'm like a fish out of water in this demographic of my community. I don't fit in, and I don't know where to start." In actuality, you don't have to worry about where you start; God will show you, just like he showed Dr. Esther Turner how to minster in her community.

In the 1950s, Dr. Turner was a white professor at Cascade College in Portland. She had a great career as a professor, but she was burdened for the African American children she saw in the community. At that time it was uncommon for a white person to reach out to a predominately African American part of the community. As her burden grew, she convinced a few of the other professors to help her conduct Bible studies and activities for the children. The more she engaged and was present with the children, the more her burden and desire to do more grew. Eventually, the children's parents began inquiring about the Lord, and she decided to form a church.

The name of the church was Immanuel Interracial Free Methodist Church. The name alone says a mouthful. The first word is *Immanuel*, meaning God with us. God is with us, and indirectly we are with God and one another. The second word, *interracial*, spoke of the societal, community and racial barriers to be overcome for the church to be formed. Third, *Free Methodist*—it was the only Free Methodist church in a predominately African American community.

It is now almost sixty years later, and the church still exists. It's reaching out to the community but has much room for improvement. Although it has undergone some major shifts since it was founded, it still has Dr. Turner's heartbeat to minister to the community. The missional value to be present is a part of its DNA.

Here's a reality check: God doesn't always call us to serve in comfortable places. Sometimes he calls you and me to serve in areas that stretch us. That being the case, as followers of Jesus we go where he leads, no matter the discomfort. We need to be willing to navigate the path and the relationships so we can reach our ministry destination.

You may have served for years in a particular location or ministry in your community, only to wake up one morning and discover that the community has changed, and you are now the stranger in a once familiar place. If that's the case, what do you do? Jump ship? Absolutely not! If you believe God still has work for you or your church to do in that place, renew your effort to navigate through the once familiar territory.

These days, almost everybody has access to a GPS, whether it's a special feature in a car or an app on a smartphone. Simply entering an address and pushing a button guides you turn by turn to where you want to go. If only navigating into your community was as easy as pushing a button! However, you can use a good set of "navigational wills" (or wheels) to help you reach your ministry destination in your community.

But before we talk more about them, let me mention briefly why they're important and how they're going to help you navigate in your community. There's a word you may or may not be familiar with: *exegesis* (pronounced *eksijēsis*). Exegesis is the process of thoroughly studying a Bible text using language, history, context and other tools to come to an accurate explanation and interpretation of a passage. The origin of the word *exegesis* is a Greek word meaning to guide or lead out. When people exegete a text, they pull out its true meaning instead of simply conjuring up their own interpretation.

Navigating your community requires you to be an exegete—that is, you have to take the journey into your community and use the proper tools in order to understand your community and its needs so that you can accurately interpret your course of action for ministry.

Now that we've had a little Theology 101, let's get to the navigational wills so we can get moving.

The Will to Get Unstuck

I'm in the process of learning how to navigate my own community again. I basically grew up in Portland and went to high school here, and in the years when my family lived in Bellevue, Washington, 99 percent of our vacations were to Portland. In 1988, when I became the pastor of Life Change, I knew our community like the back of my hand. Without exaggeration, if I went to a grocery store, I would know almost all the workers and the shoppers. A trip to the store was not only a grocery trip but also a meet-and-greet event.

Although the mission of our church has always been to be racially diverse, the demographic of our neighborhood has been primarily African American. In some places, if you saw a white person or Latino walking through the neighborhood, you would wonder if he or she was lost. North and northeast Portland was our community, and I knew how to navigate it.

Fast-forward to 2014, and, oh man, things have changed! If you're my age, you probably remember the song that starts, "Oh where, oh where has my little dog gone? Oh where, oh where can he be?" Well, I've got an adaptation: "Oh where, oh where has my community gone? Oh where, oh where can it be?" I can't tell where it's gone, but I can sure tell you where it isn't. It isn't where it used to be!

Our neighborhood and community have been completely gentrified. Dilapidated buildings and quite a few vacant houses once surrounded our church. Now we sit on the hottest strip of real estate in the city of Portland. When I used to tell people how to find our church, I would just say, "Make a right on Williams Avenue, and you can't miss us. Our church is the big building that sits between Williams and Vancouver." That's not the case now. Our building is dwarfed by new construction. I even hear comments now from people saying that it's hard to find our church; they can't even see it in the midst of all the new development.

The new buildings are not the only things that have changed. The residents of our community have as well. North and northeast Portland are no longer primarily African American. It has become a white community that is very expensive to live in. Today seeing a black person walking or driving in the community is strange. I bumped into one of my high school friends, who has been living in another city for the past ten years, at the new organic market down the street from the church. He was in shock; he could not wrap his brain around the change that had taken place. He did all the talking as I sat there listening to him sigh and watching him shake his head in disbelief.

A friend of mine came and preached at our church. He hadn't preached there in several years, so he too was amazed by all the changes. His exact words were, "You must be really excited with the renaissance that's taking place in your community. This is so cool!" I must have had a tense look on my face, because he quickly added, "You're happy about this. This is a good thing, right?" I just nodded and gave a plastic smile.

Our whole community as we knew it is gone, vanished, no more. We've got hundreds of white hipsters as neighbors, most of whom walk past us as if we don't even exist. I feel the daily sting of seeing white developers erecting their dreams on soil we envisioned occupying in our dreams. I feel the frustration of people having no place to park for church on Sunday because the once-vacant places on the street are filled with the hybrid cars of those eating at the dozen or more niche restaurants that line our streets.

I feel anger because the once flagship high school in our community is now sinking into a grave due to the gentrification that has occurred. Families have lost their homes. African American businesses have evaporated. So there is no way I call this a renaissance. I call it grand theft! Who in the world is happy after they've been robbed?

Such was my dilemma: Our church was still in this community. I knew without a doubt God loves every white person and every hipster on the block. I knew his desire was for each one of them to know Jesus and become a part of his family. But at the time I wasn't much good, because I was grieving the loss of our community. In my view, we were the Hatfields, and they were the McCoys.

I was battling with some real internal issues. But even with my heart condition, a merger was going to happen. God had to give me the will to get over my pain and disappointment so I could get unstuck and begin to navigate my new surroundings. And he did!

In Acts 10:9-16, God got the apostle Peter unstuck so he could make his way to Caesarea to participate in a Jesus collision. There was a Gentile man named Cornelius living in Caesarea. He was seeking God, and in answer to his prayer, God instructed him to send for Peter, who was some thirty miles away in Joppa. God's plan was for Peter to go and preach the gospel to Cornelius and his household so that they could receive the Holy Spirit. So, in response to God's leading, Cornelius sent a delegation to bring Peter back to Caesarea.

To make this collision possible, God had to reach Peter before the delegation arrived at the house where he was staying. God had to push him past the racial, cultural and religious issues that would have kept him from journeying into Cornelius's community. If that delegation had reached Peter before God got him unstuck, there was no way on earth he would have left Joppa and gone with them. Here's what God did:

> About noon the following day as they were on their journey and approaching the city, Peter went up on the roof to pray. He became hungry and wanted something to eat, and while the meal was being prepared, he fell into a trance. He saw heaven opened and something like a large sheet being let down to earth by its four corners. It contained all kinds of four-footed animals, as well as reptiles of the earth and birds of the air. Then a voice told him, "Get up, Peter. Kill and eat."
>
> "Surely not, Lord!" Peter replied. "I have never eaten anything impure or unclean."
>
> The voice spoke to him a second time, "Do not call anything impure that God has made clean." (Acts 10:9-15)

This happened three times, and immediately the sheet was taken back to heaven. Peter was so stuck that God had to convey the message three times before he finally got it. The message was that God is after every soul, not just Jewish souls. And Peter clearly got it, because he would later say to the delegation, "You are well aware that it is against our law for a Jew to associate with a Gentile or visit him. But God has shown me that I should not call any man impure or unclean" (Acts 10:28).

A few years back, I was in my office, talking to God about our community and the changes that were happening. While I was praying, I got a picture in my mind of a chessboard with a game still in progress. The sky didn't open up like it did for Peter; it was just a picture in my mind. (That's kind of how I think, with pictures.) While I was thinking about this picture, I clearly heard the Lord speak these words to my heart: "I am sovereign."

In an instant, chains broke from around my heart and soul. I no longer felt as if God had failed us or abandoned our community. I was assured that every single movement that had taken place in our community—every movement on the chessboard—and all of those to come were under the superintendence of God. In those few minutes, I was freed to begin navigating my new community and working with God to see some incredible collisions take place. And besides that, I could now work with the Lord to get our church unstuck, because they, too, were dealing with anger about changes in the community.

What's your unstuck story? Maybe it's fear or a hurt you've experienced. Honestly pour your heart out to God. In his wisdom, God will give you what you need to make you mobile. If you have the willingness to be unstuck, God will see to it that you are.

The Will to Make the Journey

Once you're unstuck, you have a willingness to make the journey. Once Peter was freed from his personal hang-ups, that willingness to journey was woven into the fabric of his soul. The Spirit said to him, "Simon, three men are looking for you. So get up and go downstairs. Do not hesitate to go with them, for I have sent them" (Acts 10:19-20). God doesn't help us get unstuck so we stay where we are. He frees us so that we can take the journey to the spot where he's calling us to serve.

The truth about a journey is just that: it's a journey. You're not going to arrive there in one day or maybe even in one year. Peter had to travel thirty miles to reach Caesarea. It wasn't an afternoon stroll in the park. He had some ground to cover, and it took him time to walk it.

Journeying into your community isn't a matter of physical miles; it's a matter of relational miles. So settle into the fact that reaching your destination requires time. Anyone can get on a plane and travel halfway around the world in less than twenty-four hours. To do that, all you need is money. Relational miles require more than money. They are racked up by building credibility and trust within your community. They come from you being willing to do the same old repetitive trot, being present and loving to your neighbor, day by day, week by week, month by month and year by year.

It's like a friend of mine who does community work to help disenfranchised people told me: "When I first started, no one really listened to me or took me seriously. Now, after several years, I'm considered an expert." In essence, he kept walking, and he's having an impact in his community.

Here are a couple of pieces of advice regarding your willingness to journey:

- You're not alone; lean on God for support and strength. With every step you take into unfamiliar territory, he is with you.

- Stay willing to journey. I guarantee that you will hit bumps in the road that will make you want to quit. Don't allow these momentary tests to derail you. Grow through them and learn. Allow the same willingness you possessed to begin the journey remain throughout the journey.

- Keep the goal in mind. Remember, you are taking a journey to share Jesus with your community. Imagine the transformation in the lives of those people if you journey well. With that in mind, keep on truckin'!

The Will to Be Guided

One of the ways to navigate your way around a city you are unfamiliar with is to acquire the services of a tour guide. A knowledgeable tour guide has information about the city that will help you to acclimate as well as give you some idea of where you may venture off to next. If you're feeling God's leading to engage your community in an area you're unfamiliar with—or, as in my case, you're surrounded by an entirely different demographic—enlist the service of a guide. Peter needed a guide to reach the place where God was leading him. Listen to this:

> Peter went down and said to the men, "I'm the one you're looking for. Why have you come?"
>
> The men replied, "We have come from Cornelius the centurion. He is a righteous and God-fearing man, who is respected by all the Jewish people. A holy angel told him to have you come to his house so that he could hear what you have to say." Then Peter invited the men into the house to be his guests.

The next day Peter started out with them, and some of the brothers from Joppa went along. The following day he arrived in Caesarea. Cornelius was expecting them and had called together his relatives and close friends. (Acts 10:21-24)

God's plan was for Peter to merge into Cornelius's space, but in order for him to make the journey, he needed help from some trustworthy guides.

My friend Rick McKinley has been a very helpful guide in my attempt to navigate through our changed community. Rick is a white soul brother. Like me, he has a heart to see the gospel impact our entire city, penetrating all racial and socio-economic barriers. Besides that, Rick knows the demographic that now lives around our church community. He has pastored that slice of the population for over twelve years and has lived in their world.

It's not so much that our conversations are about him telling me to do X, Y and Z; rather, it's me learning from him their value system, their worldviews and their culture. He also has helped me not merely to look at what I'm seeing but to understand why I'm seeing it. He has helped me to gain a better understanding of the needs of the new hipster crowd and of what it takes to reach then.

While I still have a long way to go, Rick's guidance has made me more comfortable with my community and helped me to move miles forward in my journey. He has helped me to navigate better. As a result, our church is becoming increasingly diverse. We are praying and strategizing diligently to find more ways to fit into the current neighborhood context while at the same time staying true to our core convictions and values. It's definitely a challenge, but it's fun too.

Where are you trying to go in your community? Do you hope to change policies that adversely affect the underprivileged? Do you want to reach girls caught in sex trafficking? Is your passion to create a business in your community that gives a gospel witness? Wherever you are trying to go, find guides to help your cause. They have been where you are, and they are where you want to go.

Where can you find them? Right under your nose! Chances are that God has placed people in your path to help you. This is God's idea anyway, not yours or mine. Just as God was faithful to give Peter the guides he needed, he will provide for you.

The Will to Learn from Your Neighbors

Navigating your community also requires you to be a learner. Part of our problem in our zeal to help is that we make the assumption that we have all the answers before we even understand the situation. In the words of my cousin Pat, "Who does that?" Me and maybe you!

Think about this: Jesus' public ministry likely started when he was about thirty. What was he doing all those previous years? Being human, getting a firsthand experience of what life is like for you and me. He tasted the trials, the joys and the heartbreaks that accompany the human experience. Let's face it, Jesus is God—he could have fixed our human predicament any way he desired. But he chose to learn from his human experience first. He grew in wisdom and understanding with God and man (Luke 2:52). He learned obedience from the things he suffered (Hebrews 5:8). If Jesus learned from his ministry context, we can definitely learn from ours.

Let's go back to Peter. When he reached Cornelius's house, he was in learner mode. Though God had used him remarkably in other places, he didn't project his past ministry experiences and successes onto the new situation. He was eager to learn about Cornelius's heartfelt needs and concerns. Here's the account of how it went down; note Peter's willingness to learn as well as what he learned:

> Peter went inside and found a large gathering of people. He said to them: "You are well aware that it is against our law for a Jew to associate with a Gentile or visit him. But God has shown me that I should not call any man impure or unclean. So when I was sent for, I came without raising any objection. May I ask why you sent for me?"
>
> Cornelius answered: "Four days ago I was in my house praying at this hour, at three in the afternoon. Suddenly a man in shining clothes stood before me and said, 'Cornelius, God has heard your prayer and remembered your gifts to the poor. Send to Joppa for Simon who is called Peter. He is a guest in the home of Simon the tanner, who lives by the sea.' So I sent for you immediately, and it was good of you to come. Now we are all here in the presence of God to listen to everything the Lord has commanded you to tell us." (Acts 10:27-33)

By listening to Cornelius, Peter learned exactly what he needed and was perfectly positioned to deliver.

There's a young hipster who works at a store I frequent. When I first saw this young man, I was tempted to share the Four Spiritual Laws to try to lead him to Christ, simply because that's the way I'm used to sharing Christ with strangers. But it didn't feel right.

For months, our conversation consisted only of him asking for my order, but over the last couple of years, he has started to share some details of his life with me. At his own initiative, we've had conversations about church, and when something major in his life is going on, he fills me in. It has taken a while, but a bridge has been built. If I had used some of my old-school evangelistic methods, which I still use from time to time, I would have turned him off, and the door would have been shut.

Now, because of him, God is helping me to build bridges with others in the store too. It's funny, because when I go there with my daughter, they'll yell greetings from behind the counter. My daughter then gives me the teenager look that says, "Dad, how in the world do they know your name?" I tell her it's because Dad, with God's help, has been learning how to navigate in a changed community, and he is learning to get to know new people. Her enthusiastic response is, "Whatever!"

There's a saying we have in the hood that goes like this: "If you don't know, you better ask somebody!" To put it another way, if you want to navigate successfully in your community, learn all you can from the people you are seeking to reach so that you can minister to them effectively.

The Will to Give What You Have

This last navigational will is the merger tipping point (we'll discuss this more in depth in chapter ten, "Super-Simple Plan"). This is the main reason you navigated your way through the community. It's the sole purpose behind your tedious journey. You didn't come this far to whiff and not deliver the goods you're supposed to deliver. You are now in the very spot where you can freely give what God has given you to share.

The goal of Peter's journey was to share the gospel with Cornelius and his household. Acts 10:34-43 tells us that's exactly what Peter did; he delivered the goods. He gave the eager listeners a historical account of Jesus' life, mission, death and resurrection. While he was telling the gospel story, the Spirit of God fell on the Gentiles just as he fell on the Jews at the day of Pentecost. They all believed in Jesus and were baptized.

The implications of what happened from that one journey are enormous. The collision at Cornelius's home helped set the precedent for Jesus collisions to happen in Gentile homes all over the world.

Jesus said, "And if anyone gives even a cup of cold water to one of these little ones because he is my disciple, I tell you the truth, he will certainly not lose his reward" (Matthew 10:42). You don't have to be some great religious leader with an impressive résumé and credentials to be able to offer something needful to your community. If God, in his sovereignty, has orchestrated your steps in your community and placed you before an audience, he has given you something to give. Even if what you have is only a cup of cold water, that cup of water you hold in your hand is exactly what God wants them to receive, because it is what he gave you to give to them. Don't fall into the "I don't have anything to offer" trap; you have something to give—so give it! As in the case of Peter, these people are waiting on you to come, and they are ready to receive.

Navigating through your community will require time and effort. You must be willing to do what it takes to get unstuck, to take the journey and to be guided in order to learn and to give what God has given you. If you do so, your navigation will direct you to the heart of your community destination. You may end up being totally surprised at the outcomes God accomplishes through your journey simply because you paid the price to get there.

For Reflection and Discussion

1. What destination is God leading you to in your community?

2. What issues or attitudes are preventing you from making the journey?

3. Do you think you need the help of a navigational guide? If so, who might you reach out to for help?

4. What gift do you believe God would have you share with your community?

5. How will you pray for your journey and your church's journey into your community?

SIX

A Towel or a Title

When you serve your community, you bring to the table more than just your gifts, talents and passions. Accompanying you on the journey is a make-or-break passenger called attitude. Having the right attitude toward the community you serve is a nonnegotiable point. Why? For one, your attitude will be a huge factor in people determining if they want what you're offering or not. Two, as a follower of Jesus Christ, your gift to the community is more than just goods and services. Your ultimate goal is to make Jesus visible and accessible to those you are serving. Serving your community with the wrong attitude hides Jesus in a dense fog of mistrust, a fog that makes it difficult for the ones you are serving to see and reach him.

What's a right attitude? What's a wrong attitude? You and I both know answering that question can provoke a long conversation, but the late John Garlington explains it beautifully. Garlington was a beloved pastor and wonderful servant of Jesus Christ in our community. He not only preached about having a right attitude, he lived it. Here's his philosophy: "Authentic service to Jesus in the church and in the community requires you to take a towel and not a title." When you do this, you are expressing an act of love and worship toward the one you follow—Jesus Christ. By taking a towel and not a title, you are exemplifying the servant model Jesus himself gave us to follow.

In John 13, we are privileged to see a revolutionary moment in the lives of Jesus and his disciples. It is revolutionary in the sense that by a single act of servitude, Jesus dismantles and turns upside-down the popular notion of upward mobility. In a real-life model, he shows his disciples that the power to produce kingdom transformation lies in a piece of cloth called a towel. He makes it clear that our job is to serve and not to be served. In addition, our preoccupation should not be ourselves but others. Jesus models this beautifully to his disciples.

It was the last meal Jesus was going to eat with his disciples before his crucifixion. Though the disciples had learned a lot from him, they were in the dark about a number of things. For one, they had no idea that Satan had won over Judas's heart and that in a matter of hours he would sell out Jesus for thirty piece of silver. Had they known, Judas would probably not have been able to leave that room the same way he entered it. They were equally blind to their primary roles as disciples. Knowing this, Jesus did something unheard of to make sure his boys got the message loud and clear.

Before Jesus spoke the message he wanted the disciples to hear, he modeled it. He got up from the table, took off his outer clothing, put a towel around his waist and poured water in a basin. On his knees, he began to wash each of the disciples' feet with the water in the basin and dry them with his towel. Repulsed by Jesus' actions, Peter told Jesus, "You shall never wash my feet." To which Jesus replied, "Unless I wash you, you have no part with me" (John 13:8). See, neither Peter nor the other disciples understood what Jesus was doing. It was a foreign paradigm to them, and it is to many of us.

Jesus turned the master-servant roles upside down. He showed his disciples that their call in life was not to be masters and lords over people but to be humble servants. He was teaching them that the authority and power they had received from him were not so they would wield a title, but so they would lovingly serve. After Jesus modeled the behavior and attitude the disciples were to embrace, he said to them,

> You call me "Teacher" and "Lord," and rightly so, for that is what I am. Now that I, your Lord and Teacher, have washed your feet, you also should wash one another's feet. I have set you an example that you should do as I have done for you. I tell you the truth, no servant is greater than his master, nor is a messenger greater than the one who sent him. Now that you know these things, you will be blessed if you do them. (John 13:13-17)

If anyone could have been title-driven, it would have been Jesus. Think about it for a moment: Who do you and I know that can truthfully be called the King of kings, the Lord of lords and the Alpha and Omega? Absolutely no one—except Jesus. Although that was the case, Jesus put aside the majesty that was rightfully his and instead used the power that was given to him to serve and empower those who were lesser. His selfless act demonstrates the posture and the attitude we are to have as we engage our community.

Towelology 101

The question we have to grapple with is, how did Jesus have the freedom to use a towel and wash the feet of a not-so-clean group of guys? Or, what decision must we make and what values do we need to espouse in order to have a servant's heart and attitude? Zeroing in on several of Jesus' actions and words in this story will give a great answer. I call it Towelolgy 101.

Lesson 1: Be clear on the differences between a towel-based and a title-based attitude. This little chart helps bring some clarification.

The difference between a towel-driven attitude and a title-driven attitude

Towel-Driven Attitude	Title-Driven Attitude
Uses power and God-given gifts to empower others	Uses power and God-given gifts as a means to be served rather than to serve
Sees the intrinsic value of every person and understands all are loved by God and made in his image	Sees people as a means to an end and places low value on their worth and welfare
Recognizes that entry into a person's life is a privilege and gift from God	Believes their own presence is a gift to other people
Understands that being a servant is the way of the kingdom of God	Sees serving as a way to build their own kingdom
Honors Jesus Christ	Honors self
Has the right disposition to change lives and communities	Has the wrong disposition to change lives and communities

Lesson 2: Use your power to empower others. John 13:3 says, "Jesus knew that the Father had put all things under his power, and that he had come from God and was returning to God." Jesus did not deny the fact that he had power and privilege. God the Father had put all things under his reign; he had come from God and was returning back to God. All the power in the universe was at his disposal, and he could have had or done anything he wished. However, he chose to use his power to deepen the spiritual formation in the lives of those he loved, the ones he was serving.

You and I have power that God has given to us. Perhaps that power is in the form of influence, finances, gifts or talents. The question is, how will we use our power? Will we harness it and use it solely for our own purpose, or will we do like Jesus and use it to empower the lives of others? If we are to forge a servant's attitude into our hearts and minds, we will follow Jesus' example and empower others when we have the opportunity to do so.

Lesson 3: Relinquish your position. John 13:4 tells us, "So he got up from the meal [and] took off his outer clothing." Serving your community with the right attitude requires you to relinquish something. Jesus relinquished two forces that prohibit service. The first was his seat at the table, and the second was his clothing. Jesus knew he would not have the mobility to bend down and wash the feet of the disciples if he stayed seated at the table. To wash the disciples' feet, he had to forfeit his position. He also knew his outer garments were not conducive to washing feet, so he took them off in order to be unrestricted and to serve.

We all have tables and garments that prevent us from having the mobility needed to serve our communities. Those tables or restrictive garments can be our jobs, our socioeconomic status, our beliefs or values, our past experiences or even our theology. And, I might add, our fears or our race. However, if we follow Jesus' example, there is a power available to us that will strengthen us to unseat ourselves from any table. The power is called love. Jesus loved his disciples to the point that he humbled himself, moved from the table and served. Love for our community will compel us to move from behind the table, unwrap our garments and lovingly wash the feet of our community. We joyfully relinquish our positions because Jesus loves, and we love our community!

Lesson 4: Value those you serve. Jesus loved his disciples, and that love for them motivated him to give them his all. "Having loved his own who were in the world, he now showed them the full extent of his love" (John 13:1). When you truly love the community you serve, your goal is to give, not take. Title-driven people take from the community, but servants give to the community. Our communities are full of takers on the streets, in corporations and, in many cases, in political offices. My friend JO pastors Heart of the City Church in Coeur d'Alene, Idaho, which has tentacles reaching throughout their entire city. It reaches out to businesses and feeds the poor and hungry. It is a church that truly lives between Bethel and Ai. Its motto is "We give because we love!" If you are a true lover, you will be a true giver.

Lesson 5: Don't let one bad apple spoil the whole bucket. Being a servant and having the right attitude doesn't mean everyone you serve is going to love or respect you for what you do. When the bad apple surfaces, you'll feel tempted to trash the whole bucket. You might ask yourself, *What's the use? Nobody is appreciating my sacrifices and hard work. All I'm getting out of this deal is a kick from the very feet I have washed with my own hands.* Friend, don't feel bad when you experience this. Don't forget, Jesus washed the feet of Judas, the one who would shortly betray him. The truth is that in the fabric of servanthood, there is a strand of suffering. However, God does not allow the suffering you experience to derail you from your mission but to forge in you a deeper reliance on him for the grace to sustain you and keep you in the fight. Don't let one bad apple ruin your entire harvest.

Lesson 6: Be a copycat. I had just finished teaching a Bible class on a Wednesday night and was walking down the hall to close up my office and go home for the night when I saw Trevor, a three- or four-year-old boy, walking down the hall to meet me. His eyes were as wide as Frisbees, and he was holding a red rope licorice that he had taken off the desk in my office. It was hilarious! But I couldn't let him get away with taking licorice off my desk without permission, could I?

I cornered him and asked, "Trevor, did you take that licorice off my desk without asking?" I may as well have been speaking Greek, the way he stared at me like a deer in headlights, so I said, "Trevor, before you take my licorice, you should say, 'Pastor Mark, can I have a piece of your licorice?'" He nodded but said nothing. I repeated myself. Then he said, "Pastor Mark, can I have a piece of your licorice? You have to ask before you take something off my desk."

I got a good laugh out of that, and I also learned that Trevor is a great copycat. Jesus set the example for us on how to be a servant, and he tells us to be copycats of him, saying, "Now that I, your Lord and Teacher, have washed your feet, you also should wash one another's feet. I have set you an example that you should do as I have done for you" (John 13:14-15). Like little Trevor, you and I get to copy Jesus, not just verbally but from our hearts.

If we listen to what Jesus said abut servanthood and follow the example he set for us, we will joyfully grab a towel and venture into our communities. We will possess the right attitude to bring transformation and life to those around our community table. To bring the reality of this point even closer to home, I want to tell you a couple of stories.

A Tale of Two Servers

Someone told me this story about a scenario that happened in their community. Ted (not his real name) was a very gifted man whose passion appeared to be to impact his community for Christ. He was creative and full of ideas and energy, and the church he was working with was very excited about what he brought to the table. For a few months, he talked with community members and church members in order to devise a plan for community engagement. The plan of action was to meet the felt needs of the community by providing certain goods and services.

Everything was going great until it became "Show Time—Today, Live with Ted." When the lights came on, it became obvious to the church and the community that Ted had a title agenda, not a towel agenda. All of a sudden he had become the authority on what the church should be doing. The rightness of the church's plan of action could be validated only if it was suitable to his palate. He would argue with people, expressing his opinions and views without respect for others. He even rubbed the community the wrong way. It was hosting an event similar in nature to what Ted desired to do, but he decided to do his own thing on the same day instead.

The person who was telling me this story was miffed. "Mark," she said, "this guy is getting on everybody's nerves—the church and the city! We all just want him out of here. For Jesus' sake, he needs to go!" And go he did. They ran him out of town like he was Jesse James. In reality, it was not that extreme, but he definitely got the message that the title stuff wasn't suitable for the church or the community. He was hurting both places.

What makes this situation so disheartening is that if Ted had had the right attitude, he could have made a major impact in the community. Everybody was willing to work with him, but his attitude sabotaged the wonderful work that could have occurred. Sadly, he's in a new place doing the same thing again.

I admit this example seems extreme, but I have seen title seekers with way more couth than Ted. It doesn't matter how well they hide it or how slick they are, their title attitudes eventually surface—and when they do, no one profits. Neither the person nor the church and the community will benefit.

On a brighter note, Stefon and Marcie Spruill are and have been a tremendous blessing to our church and to our community for years. The church employs neither Stefon nor Marcie, and their ministry is not funded or initiated by the church. They both have full-time jobs, but they feel a call to serve the community. For seven years, every Monday—whether rain, sleet, snow or sunshine—from eight to noon, Stefon and Marcie set up three tents on the corner of Garfield and Failing. To put it mildly, Garfield and Failing were not the place you would want to have a family picnic. On that street was a combination of apartments and houses that were riddled with drug abuse, prostitution and mental health issues.

Using their own money, the Spruills bought food and prepared a hot meal for anyone who wanted something to eat. They would set the food up under the tents, and hungry souls could come and eat, receive prayer and talk about the Bible if they wanted to.

The majority of the people that the Spruills served were deep into their addictions, and they loved the pair and appreciated what they were doing. Over the course of those seven years, they fed more than five thousand people and led many people to Christ. Now much of the chaos that was present in that place has subsided. The Spruills certainly had their share of heartbreaks and disappointments, but their love for the people compelled them to keep on serving Monday after Monday.

Stefon and Marcie are truly towel bearers. Their goal wasn't to achieve a title; they just wanted to serve like Jesus. They called their ministry to Garfield and Failing "On the Block Ministry," and their mission statement was "To love, encourage and embrace those who are lost, compelling them to come into the kingdom of God by following Jesus' example of love."

According to Stefon, the verse that fueled their mission was Luke 14:23: "Then the master told his servant, 'Go out to the roads and country lanes and make them come in, so that my house will be full.'"

When you make your merger with your community, arrive not only with your gifts and talents but also with a servant's heart and attitude. To accomplish what Jesus wants, you will have to go in like Stefon and Marcie: with the servant's towel firmly in your grip.

For Reflection and Discussion

1. Why do you think people are title-driven?

2. Have you ever worked with someone who is all about titles? Describe your experience.

3. How do you think you would have responded if you were at the table with the disciples and Jesus washed your feet?

4. In your own words, explain why a servant attitude toward your community is essential. How can you develop a servant posture in your own life and ministry?

5. What are some ways you can pray for yourself and your church so that you can embrace the servant's heart Jesus desires you to have?

seven

Praying for Your Community

There is a short, powerful but sad verse tucked away in the book of Ecclesiastes: "Now there lived in that city a man poor but wise, and he saved the city by his wisdom. But nobody remembered that poor man" (Ecclesiastes 9:15). What's important here is that the poor man possessed the wisdom to save his city. Think for a moment about what that means. Because the city was saved, families and homes were not destroyed, children could experience security and joy, and life was the order of the day, not death. Our communities are in need of saving from the debilitating forces of poverty, injustice, divorce, perversion and more. Finding *wisdom* is a key to helping your community experience God's restoring and redeeming love.

It is important for you to understand that God is not expecting you or your church to do everything. However, he does intend for you to do something. To discover what that special something is, a mega dose of his wisdom is needed. An infusion of his wisdom into your heart and mind can show you what he's asking you to do and give you the steps for proceeding. And God is faithful to give you all the wisdom you need so that you can do exactly what he desires you to do.

City Harvest and Single Mothers

City Harvest Church in Vancouver, Washington received God's wisdom for its community and went to work. Bob Macgregor, its pastor, grew up in a single-parent home under difficult circumstances. His mother was a hoarder and suffered from schizophrenia. Her illnesses caused Bob much pain and heartache. The Lord has done an amazing redeeming work in Bob's life, including creating compassion in Bob's heart for single mothers and their children.

City Harvest is a church that prays for their community. They spend time seeking the Lord's face, looking for his direction about community engagement. Out of Pastor Bob's heart and God's gracious wisdom, they have created an incredible ministry to single mothers in their community. Pastor Bob says, "City Harvest church targets single mothers. Single mothers and children are our mission field." They have seen many single mothers in their community come to Christ and be baptized.

City Harvest is not just after these moms making a decision for Christ, although that is extremely important. The church's members are committed to helping these moms grow and become the women God intends them to be. Their strategy includes the following:

- They work from a database collected by City Harvest Church with all the names of single mothers in their church. They began by hosting a free oil-change day for single mothers and collected the names of all the mothers who participated. They then intentionally reached out to the families on that list.

- They offer twelve weeks of parenting classes for single mothers. The women eat and share their stories and grow in community, faith and love.

- They do an event called "Mommy, It's Your Turn." Kids are dropped off at the church for a carnival while mothers go to buy something for themselves with a store gift card furnished by the church and the store.

- Once these moms come to faith in Christ, they are assigned a family in the church. That family then assists the single mother and her kids however they can.

City Harvest could have taken multiple paths in community ministry, but they made ministry to single moms a priority. In answer to their prayers, God gave the church members the wisdom and creativity to meet a pressing need in their community.

Just Ask

God is generous, freely giving his wisdom to anyone who asks. No person in the Bible ever asked God for wisdom and did not receive it. You have to understand something: God loves our communities more than you or I do. If your request to him is for wisdom to reach people whom he sent his son to die for, there is no doubt he will help you. James 1:5 says, "If any of you lacks wisdom, he should ask God, who gives generously to all without finding fault, and it will be given to him."

King Solomon asked God for wisdom to lead God's people. His prayer was answered with a downpour of wisdom from heaven, making him the wisest man on earth. His prayer to God for wisdom was simple, from the heart and to the point: "Give me wisdom and knowledge, that I may lead this people, for who is able to govern this great people of yours?" (2 Chronicles 1:10). God responded,

> Since this is your heart's desire and you have not asked for wealth, riches or honor, nor for the death of your

enemies, and since you have not asked for a long life but for wisdom and knowledge to govern my people over whom I have made you king, therefore wisdom and knowledge will be given you. And I will also give you wealth, riches and honor, such as no king who was before you ever had and none after you will have. (2 Chronicles 1:11-12)

Solomon asked God for wisdom, and God graciously gave it to him—and more.

One of my favorite passages that speaks of God being a generous giver of his wisdom is Proverbs 2:1-6:

> My son, if you accept my words
>   and store up my commands within you,
> turning your ear to wisdom
>   and applying your heart to understanding,
> and if you call out for insight
>   and cry aloud for understanding,
> and if you look for it as for silver
>   and search for it as for hidden treasure,
> then you will understand the fear of the LORD
>   and find the knowledge of God.
> For the LORD gives wisdom,
>   and from his mouth come knowledge and understanding.

There's no rocket-science degree needed here—God's wisdom is available to you for the asking. God tells you to ask for his wisdom because he wants desperately to give it to you. Praying about your community alleviates a mountain of guesswork and fills you with wisdom from heaven so that your marching orders into your community are clear.

Praying for Your Community

Your community needs your prayers. If you don't pray for your community, who will? Praying for you community doesn't have to be some starchy exercise that makes you perspire with religious sweat. Prayer for your community can be creative and fun.

A walk outside. A few summers ago, our prayer pastor, Odessa Mangum, felt that we needed to get out of the walls of the church and pray for our community. Our prayer group meets Monday through Friday from six to seven thirty in the morning. For two solid weeks, instead of gathering in our sanctuary as usual, we walked the streets of our community and prayed. Each morning we targeted a section of the community, and dozens of us quietly walked there, asking God to bless our community.

When we walked by schools, we prayed for the administration and the students. When we walked by drug houses, we prayed for addicts and asked God to get the drug dealers out. When we walked by businesses, we prayed for the owners to find Jesus and asked God to bless their businesses. Passing by hundreds of homes, we prayed God would pour out his grace on each of those families. We blanketed our community in prayer during those two weeks.

After our two weeks of prayer, we decided to give fruit baskets to a number of places that we'd prayed over. Two that received those baskets were the public school district office and our local police precinct. Without a lot of fanfare, a couple of the women in the prayer group delivered our gifts and told them, "We want to show you our appreciation for your hard work in our community and let you know our church is praying for you."

What has transpired over the last couple of years is amazing. Our church has become the central meeting place for discussing community issues, and the police department is always at the table. We also host a charter school in our building that is a part of Portland public schools. We went out and prayed for the community, and God brought them back to us in the church. I tell you, those prayer walks were fun, and we got some exercise in the process.

Gathering with others. For the last several years, dozens of churches and thousands of believers throughout the Greater Portland area have gathered for seven days of fasting and prayer in our city. We call it Seven. We divide the city into sections and designate a different church each night as the place where people will gather to pray. Each prayer gathering is led by a group of pastors or leaders who come from almost every denomination under the sun. It's a beautiful time of the churches coming together to pray for their city.

The night begins with worship and proceeds with several leaders sharing for three to five minutes about an issue that impacts the church or our city. Each night the church prays fervently and intelligently over five to six issues, whether they be in city hall or the lowest gutter.

Seven produces excitement in the hearts of those involved. Moving the prayer meetings around to different churches allows everyone to see each other's community. Friendships are built and wedges that separate the churches weaken and melt away. Seven is a creative way to pray for a city and community. And beyond that, God has been answering our prayers.

Your personal prayer life. In an earlier chapter we talked about Nehemiah and his passion for the community of people who lived in Jerusalem. His passion led him to initiate a great surge of community development in Jerusalem, but it also drove him to his knees.

Nehemiah was devoted to praying for his community—not just at the onset but continually. From the first chapter to the last, Nehemiah prays to God for his community and himself. We see him praying for several different things:

- Mercy and grace to alleviate the suffering in his community caused by sin and destruction (1:4-11)

- Favor and wisdom to receive permission and resources from the king so that he can go home and rebuild the city (2:1-5)

- Protection from his enemies so that God's work in his community would not be stopped (4:4-6)

- Encouragement so that he won't get weary in doing good (5:19)

- Strength so that he and the people would be strong enough to finish the work and not succumb to the intimidation and fear of their enemies (6:14)

- Relief from the hardship the people are experiencing due to sin and God's deliverance (9:32-36)

- Remembrance and favor, asking God not to forget him and acknowledging that if God doesn't sustain him, he will not be a help to the community (13:10-14)

Nehemiah is a great example of why and how we should pray for our community. For Nehemiah, prayer for his community wasn't a formula but a lifestyle.

Here are a few ways you can make praying for your community a lifestyle. In a given day you may pray while sitting, walking and standing. You may also lie down, but chances are that you won't do much praying staring at the back of your eyelids. It may be helpful to have a set of keys you can use through the day when praying:

- *Sitting*—the key to concentration. Make a prayer list that you can use when you're sitting down to pray. On that list, include prayer points for yourself as they relate to your community. Also list prayer points for the people that live in your community as well as the issues that impact them. This takes away any guesswork about what you are going to pray for. You will know that when you sit down and pray for you community, you and God will discuss the prayer points on your sheet.

- *Walking*—the key to observation. When you walk, ride your bike or drive through your community, open your eyes. Look at people's faces, hear their voices, smell the smells and pray for your community. Ask God to bless the couple you see walking down the street. Pray for Jesus to collide with the young man you see who seems to have lost his way. Pray for the businesses and owners as you walk by. When you see or hear something that strikes a chord in your heart, pray.

- *Standing*—the key to inspiration. Sometimes you will find yourself in a situation where you are required to act, almost like Nehemiah standing before the king. When King Xerxes asked him what was wrong, he couldn't retreat to pray. He had to pray right then and there, standing on his feet. When you're in your community, having a conversation, and someone needs help, impromptu prayers in the quietness of your heart are great. The Spirit of God living in you can place on your heart what to ask the Father, and God can and may answer your prayer while you are standing in that very spot.

God wants you to make prayer for your community a part of your lifestyle. Learning to pray while you sit, walk and stand can be a helpful tool in your prayer journey. I've done this for years, so it has become second nature to me. Try it for a while, and soon praying for your community will become as natural and as necessary as breathing.

Praying with Your Community

There are times as you move about in your community that you will have God-given opportunities to pray face-to-face with the people you serve. By virtue of the relationship you have built with them, regardless of them knowing Jesus or not, they will probably allow you to pray with them. They have observed your life through the course of the relationship, and they know you care and only want the best for them. They will see your request to pray for them not as something weird or hyperreligious but as an act of love and compassion, just like everything else you do.

In cooperation with several other churches in our community, we conduct what we call a Fresh Wind service. We hold it once every quarter and rotate the meeting place from church to church. The goal of the service is to foster a greater sense of unity among the churches and to emphasize our responsibility as the church to be salt and light in our community. Through our 11:45 outreach to the community (which you'll learn more about later), we had been in the process of building relationships with a number of service agencies in our community, so we invited them to come to one particular Fresh Wind service as well. In our invitation for them, we explained that our intent was to honor and pray for them. That night we had educators, community activists and law enforcement people show up.

We wanted to make the prayer time as personal as possible, so we recognized our community guests and invited them all to come to the front of the church. Then we asked a number of people from the church who had been working in the community to come forward as well. We expressed our appreciation to our guests and thanked them for their service. We then asked those standing beside them to place a hand on a guest's shoulders.

We wanted every guest present to feel the touch of a caring human hand. We didn't rush the moment but allowed those standing to have time to pray for God's blessing on the person they were touching. While this was happening, we could see expressions on faces indicating that God was present and moving in hearts. Some of our guests were shedding tears while others were smiling. We concluded the time with a prayer from one of the pastors. At the end of the service, we thanked our guests again for coming and let them know that they would always be in our prayers and that we were there to serve them.

Sometimes when you pray with your community, you never know the impact. But on this occasion, one person let us know. He wrote,

> To the Good People of North Portland:
>
> I write to you as your public servant and a human being in awe of the outpouring of community support. I was honored to be in your presence at the Life Change Church on the evening of March 18. It has been a difficult week for the Police Bureau, having lost one of our own to shocking and confusing circumstances. The next day, we witnessed another person take their life in the middle of our North Precinct parking lot. Our day-to-day experiences can be bizarre and overwhelming, leaving us with many un-answered questions and in a state of exhaustion.
>
> I came to your service in such a condition, having had only a few hours of sleep the previous night. The workdays have been filled with chaos and unpredictability, as is typical in police work. However, there is nothing "routine"

about it, despite what we cops may say sometimes. We try to act tough, deal with things as best as we can, and stay healthy. But even those of us in the best condition cannot deny that it wears on you, takes a toll on your family, and causes you to ask yourself at times if it is all worthwhile.

And then something magical happens.

I almost didn't come last night, being tired, discouraged and worn down. I was afraid that my humanity might show through and that I would not be in my best condition. My game face was definitely not on. However, the community that I am so honored to serve accepted my presence graciously, respectfully and without judgment. Far more, in fact, you blessed me, prayed for me, and held me in high esteem. You believed in me and assumed my good intentions. I was humbled to the point of tears; your spirit of strength and inspiring voices drove me to carry on. My doubt was allayed; my resolve renewed, my passion reignited. Your faith restored my soul.

Thank you.

The forces of evil are in retreat. The dark one can no longer take our children and hijack our future. The community has united; nothing can stand in the face of victory. I implore you: continue the Good Work. Go forth, and conquer. Or as Paul, one so much more eloquent than I put it:

"Who shall separate us from the love of Christ? Shall trouble or hardship or persecution or famine or nakedness or danger or sword? . . . No, in all these things we are more than conquerors through Him who loved us."

His words of appreciation illustrate the power of what can take place when you pray with your community. There's something absolutely marvelous that happens in a person's heart when the Spirit of God ministers grace to the depth of their soul. It surpasses any human thing you or I can do or say. Those prayers communicate deeply to part of the human heart that is reserved for God and God alone.

Conclusion

Praying together doesn't have to happen during an orchestrated service. You can pray with people on the streets, at Starbucks or in homes. What's important is not so much the place where you pray but that you make three-way contact, fashioned by your hand, your friend's hand and God's hand, creating a divine merger. This is what Jesus did! He prayed with people in his community in every kind of venue imaginable: the temple, homes, street corners and even a graveyard. When he prayed, life-giving collisions happened. His disciples did the same thing, and so did the early church.

If we are going to see Jesus collisions in our communities, we should follow suit. Look forward to praying with people in your community, and when those opportunities present themselves, seize them! It's not hard; simply ask the person if it's okay for you to pray with them. If they give you permission, go for it! If they say no, accept their answer graciously and look for another opportunity.

Prayer is vital for impacting your community, so the more you can pray about, for and with your community, the better.

For Reflection and Discussion

1. What are some ministry areas where you could use a fresh infusion of God's wisdom?

2. What are the top four issues on your prayer list for your community and why?

3. What are some creative ways you can begin to pray for your community?

4. How do you think you can create more ways to pray together with your community?

5. How will you foster a greater emphasis on prayer for the community in your life and ministry as well as in your church?

eight

Depending on the Spirit

I f you have ever had the privilege of listening to an old-school African American preacher, it's likely that about three-quarters of the way through his homily, you heard him make an exuberant statement. With his eyes lifted to the heavens and a melody resonating through each word he spoke, he thundered out to the congregation, "I can feel my help coming!" When those words exited his mouth, he and the entire church shifted into another gear. As John Wesley would say, the man was set ablaze, and the congregation moved to the edges of their seats to watch him burn.

As wonderful and joyful as those divine moments are, it is important for us to understand the theological significance packed in the preacher's statement. Articulated in the words "I can feel my help coming" is a public affirmation of God's reliability and the preacher's dependence on God. God's reliability is conveyed through his faithfulness in graciously providing the pastor with the ability and strength he needs to execute his God-given task.

The truth of the matter is that in the same way the preacher needs help in the pulpit, we need help as we serve our community.

That help is the assistance of the power of the Holy Spirit to minster Jesus to those we serve.

Numerous organizations and individuals do great work in our communities. These good-hearted people work faithfully day after day and year after year to better the welfare of the disenfranchised. I say the following with the utmost respect and appreciation for all of those much-needed organizations and individuals: Our call to our community as followers of Jesus Christ is not simply to do good work but to do redeeming work as well.

Redeeming work happens only as the power of the Holy Spirit works through our lives and churches to communicate God's love and plan of redemption to our communities. Don't allow this to put a heavy load on you, because while you participate with God in doing the redeeming work in your community, he carries the lion's share of the load. The beauty is that God not only carries the lion's share, he carries you too. He is reliable, and his Spirit is present to help you. There are some remarkable ways the Holy Spirit will assist you in your ministry to your community as you depend on him.

Help with Communicating

Jesus made an incredible promise to his disciples before he ascended back to his Father: "You will receive power when the Holy Spirit comes on you; and you will be my witnesses in Jerusalem, and in all Judea and Samaria, and to the ends of the earth" (Acts 1:8). This promise to his disciples is an essential gift from heaven, an amazing gift of love providing the abilities we need to represent Jesus where we live. The promised gift is the Holy Spirit, who comes and lives within us. His indwelling presence bestows on us the power to be truth bearers, testifiers to our community and the world of the good news of Jesus and the life he offers for all. The life-giving power of the Holy Spirit deputizes you and grants you the authority to speak on behalf of Jesus. He empowers you to live like Jesus, love like Jesus and communicate the gospel of Jesus to your community.

In Acts 2, one hundred and twenty disciples were praying in an upper room on the day of Pentecost when suddenly Jesus' promise was delivered. The passage tells us that a sound like a violent wind came from heaven and filled the entire room where they were sitting. What appeared to be tongues of fire rested upon each of them, and they began to speak in languages not acquired by natural means. They all spoke as the Spirit enabled them.

> Now there were staying in Jerusalem God-fearing Jews from every nation under heaven. When they heard this sound, a crowd came together in bewilderment, because each one heard them speaking in his own language. Utterly amazed, they asked: "Are not all these men who are speaking Galileans? Then how is it that each of us hears them in his own native language? Parthians, Medes and Elamites; residents of Mesopotamia, Judea and Cappadocia, Pontus and Asia, Phrygia and Pamphylia, Egypt and the parts of Libya near Cyrene; visitors from Rome (both Jews and converts to Judaism); Cretans and Arabs— we hear them declaring the wonders of God in our own tongues!" Amazed and perplexed, they asked one another, "What does this mean?"
>
> Some, however, made fun of them and said, "They have had too much wine." (Acts 2:5-13)

What an incredible miracle! The Holy Spirit empowered every follower of Jesus in that room to speak directly to the hearts of an incredibly diverse group of people in such a way that every listener heard God's message in his or her native language.

Your community is filled with a diverse group of people. It may be diverse in ethnicity, socioeconomic levels, education and cultural background. Regardless of the diversity present where you serve in your community, the Holy Spirit can empower you with the ability to communicate the gospel to people in a way they understand.

There's a German term used in theology, *Sitz im Leben*, which means setting or situation in life. When you are filled with the Holy Spirit, you have the ability to communicate directly to people in your community exactly where they are in life. I see this when people come up to me after a service and tell me, "Pastor, you were all in my business today." My response usually is, "God knows where you live and exactly what you need to hear, and thank you, Holy Spirit, for speaking through me today."

A fire hydrant. My first experience preaching in an actual church involved a combination of the thrill of victory and the agony of defeat. Some of my family members and friends had urged me not to attempt to preach. One person told me in so many words that there was no way God had called me to preach. Another said that I stuttered too much to preach, which had an element of truth in it. A final word of discouragement came from a close friend who said that I wasn't educated enough to teach and preach yet.

I was so discouraged by those comments that I called my pastor and told him, "There's been a bit of a mix-up. God may have called you to be a preacher, but not me." So he let me off the hook.

But there was a war raging in my heart. I knew I loved people and I loved God's Word, and there was nothing else I'd rather do than share his truth with others. So I fasted and prayed for three days, asking God what I should do. In a turn of events, my friend—the same one who told me I lacked education—approached me and said, "Mark, I'm sorry for saying to you what I said. Man, you better be obedient and do what God is asking you to do." I called my pastor back and asked him if I could have a second chance at preaching. He obliged and rescheduled me to preach on a Sunday night.

Sunday night arrived, and to say I was nervous would be a gross understatement. Not only were my knees knocking, my elbows were too. Crowded into the church that night were family, friends, church members and others from the community.

I realized within a matter of minutes of beginning to speak that God had given me the gift of healing. How did I come to that realization? At least seven people had been cured of insomnia. They were all fast asleep three minutes into my message. Seeing the effect I was having on the people, I wanted nothing more than to hurry up and end my nightmare.

After eleven minutes and ten seconds I was done, finished, *kaput*. I grasped the pulpit, and in utter defeat bowed my head and prayed. I can't tell you what prayer the people were hearing, but in my heart, my prayer was *God, I will never do this again. Thank you that it's over!*

What happen as I prayed the last word is difficult for me to explain. It was as if God opened the door of my chest, placed a fire hydrant in the depth of my being and turned it on full blast. The force of it caused my head to rise up from a bowed down and defeated posture. I could actually feel the presence of God standing up inside my soul. Then the strangest thing happened. A sensitivity entered my soul, and I could sense the burdens the people in the pews were carrying. My stuttering was gone, and all the sleeping people woke up. I started talking again and continued for another fifteen minutes. People were encouraged, and some came to faith in Christ that night.

After the service, my dad, who was not a believer at the time, said to me, "Boy, who taught you how to speak like that?" Like me, Pops knew there was no way on earth I could communicate like that. And the truth of the matter is that it wasn't all me—it was the promise of the Holy Spirit being fulfilled in my life. That night, the Holy Spirit empowered me to communicate the gospel of Jesus Christ to my community.

I can hear you saying about now, "That's good for you, Mark, because preaching is your job, but I'm not a preacher, and I'm not going to stand in front of people in a church and talk." Friend, you don't have to be a pastor or in full-time Christian ministry. The fact of the matter is that God may not want you to be either. Your pulpit is behind the counter of the store where you work, the cubicle where you crunch your numbers, the classroom where you teach, the school where you attend, the gym where you work out or the place where you serve in your community. Right there in that spot the Holy Spirit will fill you with the power to communicate Jesus effectively to the audience he has given you.

Miss Collins. In our community, almost every African American male knows Miss Collins. Miss Collins was a German Christian woman who ran a daycare and communicated the love of Jesus to hundreds of young men and women in our community. The first time I met her, she looked like an old spinster right off the set of *Little House on the Prairie.* Despite her looks and her not-so-vogue attire, one thing was sure: she was full of love, and she communicated the gospel of Jesus with power. If you sit in a room full of pastors or community leaders who were raised in North Portland, three-quarters of them would credit Miss Collins with impacting their lives for Christ.

A few years back, *Christianity Today* did an article on a friend I grew up with here in Portland who is doing some remarkable work with gangs. John credited Miss Collins with being crucial to his success. Here's a snippet of the article:

> If John Canda had to credit one person for his faith and wide-reaching impact in Portland, Oregon, he would point to Grace Collins, a German Christian woman who ran Grace Collins Memorial Center, the daycare Canda attended while growing up in the 1960s on the city's northeast side.
>
> "Ms. Collins and her sisters would read us Scriptures," Canda, 46, recalls. "I remember sitting in Sunday school, and as the pastor shared Bible passages, I'd join in and recite with him, and people would look at me. It was all because of Ms. Collins."
>
> Long after needing day care, after spending days swimming at Dishman Community Center, Canda and his friends would visit Ms. Collins.
>
> "She'd have this 11½-minute Bible study for us, and her pantry was always full—chips, cookies, soda. We'd go there every summer; she'd fill the room. She was planting seeds," Canda said. Those seeds—namely, Scripture and community—have become vital to Canda's mission in Portland for the past 22 years: to curb gang violence in the city where he grew up, and to inspire others to do the same.[1]

Dozens of others in our community echo John's testimony. Miss Collins is a testament that the Holy Spirit is present to help every follower of Jesus communicate to others. He will help you speak the message and give you the boldness to do it.

Help with Overcoming Obstacles

Zechariah 4:6-7 is one of my life passages:

> So he said to me, "This is the word of the LORD to Zerubbabel: 'Not by might nor by power, but by my Spirit,' says the LORD Almighty. 'What are you, O mighty mountain? Before Zerubbabel you will become level ground. Then he will bring out the capstone to shouts of 'God bless it! God bless it!'"

These verses ignite in me confidence that no matter what mountain I'm facing—whether on a personal level or ministry level—my victory and success is not dependent on my smarts, my money, my connections or anything else within my arsenal of resources. The completion of what God wants to accomplish in my life and ministry is dependent solely on the work of the Holy Spirit, who levels mountains and empowers us to get the job done.

If you haven't figured this out yet, you will. When you're working to facilitate a Jesus collision in your community, you will face obstacles, roadblocks and mountains that could stop you in your tracks. However, no mountain is wide enough, tall enough or bad enough to withstand the leveling force of the Holy Spirit at work in your life.

In 1999, my friend Pastor Mike Servello of Utica, New York, was reading the local newspaper when he came across an article that troubled him. It explained that, due to the city's economic crunch, local shelters and food pantries would all close by midyear. This disturbing news raised a passion in Mike's heart to do something about the situation. But what could he do? And with what resources would he do it? The lack of resources was a giant mountain to their community. There was no way Mike could conquer that mountain by himself.

If you know Mike, you know that when he faces a challenge, he doesn't look to himself for the solution. He's a man who trusts the Spirit of God to work in difficult situations. Mike believed God was going to work to level the mountains and that he and his church, with the aid of the Holy Spirit, would make a Jesus collision in their city. And that's what happened.

Pastor Mike's plan was to find a warehouse building so that he could begin to help supply the existing food agencies in his community with the food they needed to service the community. That's easier said than done—a warehouse is not something the average person has on hand. But God does, and he moves *warehouse mountains* by his Spirit. Shortly into Mike's search for a warehouse, a prominent businessman in their city donated a thirty-thousand-square-foot building, and the Compassion Coalition was created.

The Compassion Coalition became the first and only warehouse to solicit, collect and distribute food, personal care supplies, paper products, furniture and diapers in the Utica, Rome and Mohawk Valley areas to help alleviate hunger and personal care needs in communities in central New York and beyond. Each month they give away one hundred thousand pounds of these goods to thousands of people.

In 2004 it became evident that an outreach of this magnitude is extremely difficult to maintain. The Compassion Coalition was running thousands of dollars in the negative. Pastor Mike decided to open a twenty-three-hundred square-foot store called Your Bargain Grocer. The store offers name-brand items at prices you can't find anywhere else. It helps the poor to purchase the food they need and have dignity in the process. The profits from the store cover the overhead of the warehouse so that both can operate debt free. What an amazing, mountain-leveling concept!

Pastor Mike took seriously the words of Jesus, "I was hungry and you fed me." And the Holy Spirit was faithful to move mountains so that he could do it.

Your vision may not be on the scale of Pastor Mike's, and it may not be a vision to feed the hungry. However, no matter the size of your vision or the focus, one thing is for sure: A mountain does not have to stop you, because the Holy Spirit is present to help.

Help with Healing

Jesus' ministry of healing in his community was multi-dimensional. He brought healing to people's minds, bodies and souls. He healed relationships and restored hope to hearts suffering in darkness. He opened the eyes of the blind and gave prisoners a new lease on life. As Peter said,

> You know the message God sent to the people of Israel, telling the good news of peace through Jesus Christ, who is Lord of all. You know what has happened throughout the province of Judea, beginning in Galilee after the baptism that John preached—how God anointed Jesus of Nazareth with the Holy Spirit and power, and how he went around doing good and healing all who were under the power of the devil, because God was with him. (Acts 10:36-38)

Also Jesus described his mission this way:

> The Spirit of the Lord is on me,
>   because he has anointed me

> to preach good news to the poor.
> He has sent me to proclaim freedom for the prisoners
>   and recovery of sight for the blind,
> to release the oppressed,
>   to proclaim the year of the Lord's favor. (Luke 4:18-19)

None of us is like Jesus, who the Bible says had the Spirit resting on him without measure. We have a limit. This means that no single one of us will ever do all he did. However, together we can do greater works (John 14:12). For that to happen, each one of us has to go about doing good and allowing the Holy Spirit to minister healing through us in the small slice of our community that we are called to serve. Just as God was faithful to anoint his Son with the Spirit, he is faithful to anoint you.

Marci Jackson is a police officer. But in my mind, her true occupation is an ambassador of Jesus Christ that brings healing to hurting people in our community. Beneath her badge lies a heart for the broken. If you talk with her for any length of time you will hear her passion and a call to come alongside her to pour oil on those who are hurting. Let me give you one example.

A young man was murdered, and the family held a vigil the following night. Marci was so burdened that this family wouldn't have pastoral care that she called me and a few other pastors to come and be present. When we arrived, the scene was chaotic and sorrowful. It was a crazy setting; the vigil was held in the parking lot of a strip club.

George, the other attending pastor, and I were like two fish out of water. We were lost and weren't sure exactly what we could do to help. Marci came over and told us to come with her. We watched as she consoled person after person, prayed with person after person, challenged person after person, and poured love on person after person. Yes, George and I talked and prayed with the crowd, but Marcie was the catalyst Jesus used that night to minister healing to the group of family and friends.

Josh and Trina have worked hard in the church and in the community for years to see God's healing come to individuals who struggle with addictions. And their story itself is one of God's healing and deliverance. In fact, it's one of those stories someone should make a movie about.

In the 1990s, Josh was a cocaine dealer in our community. His drug career ended when he and twenty-seven other drug dealers were busted by a federal sting operation. The penalty for his crime was a twelve-year sentence in federal prison. A few years into his incarceration, Josh said the only thought occupying his mind was, *I don't ever want to come to prison again.* This nagging thought forced him to find answers to make sure he never returned.

The quest for an answer drove Josh to the prison chapel, where he read books, asked questions, prayed and did some soul searching. After a year or so, God used a gospel record to reach his heart. Josh broke down in the middle of a chapel service and started weeping. He cried out to God, saying, "If you can do anything with me, I give myself to you."

Josh says, "When you are in federal prison, breaking down and crying where the other inmates can see and hear—that's something you just don't do!" But Josh didn't care; he desperately wanted God to change his life.

After his conversion, a childhood friend, Trina, wrote him a letter. They corresponded a few times, and she decided to pay him a visit, though she lived about an hour and a half away. That one visit turned into seven years of visits. For seven years, Trina traveled every weekend to the prison and visited with Josh from eight to three. At times Josh would tell her not to come, because she was tired from work and other activities, but she would show up anyway. During the course of those seven years, Trina prayed, asking, "Lord, how do I know he won't revert to the same behavior that landed him in prison when he gets out?" God answered by placing a peace in her heart, and she knew God had a plan.

While she was praying, God told Josh, "Trina is my beloved. Do not mess her over!" Josh said that this shocked him, because he didn't think God would speak in such an informal way. When Josh finished his sentence, he and Trina were married and have been together for twelve years now.

Out of the marvelous grace that God poured on Josh and Trina's lives, they have ministered under the power of the Spirit for several years, helping individuals whose lives have been ravished by all sorts of addictions. God uses them to bring healing to the broken. By God's Spirit, they are helping and have helped many find the same healing and freedom they've experienced. Your story may not be like Josh and Trina's, but your power source is identical, and you can tap into that power source too.

Tapping In

Being empowered with the Spirit for ministry to your community does not come through a formula you follow to achieve supernatural results. As a follower of Jesus Christ, you have the Holy Spirit living in you, and the power comes from cultivating a relationship as opposed to following a formula. Here are a couple of suggestions to help you immerse yourself in the Holy Spirit's power:

- *Cultivate greater sensitivity to the Spirit.* Practice quieting your heart and mind so that you can learn to discern his impulses and movements. Respond in obedience; take action when you hear him speaking to your heart. Discover what brings him joy and what grieves him. Be aware that he is always present and will never leave you.

- *Walk in the Spirit.* Walking daily in the Spirit means living each day not pursuing the gratification of your sinful nature. Life in the Spirit means being filled with the fruit of the Spirit so that your attitudes, character and behavior reflect Jesus Christ. If you live daily in the Spirit, you will be empowered to minister to your community in the power of the Spirit.

- *Pray for a fresh anointing.* There are times when you simply need to ask God to anoint you anew with the Spirit's power. In the book of Acts, there are a number of instances in which a person was filled with the Spirit and then preached, prayed or healed someone. We need a fresh touch of the Spirit's power from time to time, and God's answer to our cry is all we ask.

- *Have faith and trust that the Holy Spirit will empower you to do God's will.* Experiencing the Holy Spirit's power is not a touchy-feely thing—although it is certainly nice when the emotions are present. You do need simple, childlike faith in your heart to believe that when you are in the community trenches, the Holy Spirit *is* present to help and empower you. God said his Spirit will help you, and you must believe God will do exactly what he said.

See, friend, the gospel is not just a collection of stories and words about Jesus. It is a synthesis of God's message to a fallen world with the inherent power of the Holy Spirit to heal wounded and broken lives. When you serve your community, the Spirit is present to work beautiful miracles of healing in many different ways.

Back to the old-school African American preacher. You are standing with him in your community, boldly proclaiming, "I feel my help coming!"

For Reflection and Discussion

1. What are some ways you can create a greater sensitivity to the work of the Holy Spirit in your life?

2. Think of a time when you have experienced the Holy Spirit empowering you to share Jesus in your community. What happened?

3. What are some mountains that you are encountering in your life and ministry? How might you allow the Spirit to level these mountains?

4. Are there times you may have relied on your own strength and not the Spirit's power? Explain.

5. How will you pray for yourself and your church to experience a fresh anointing of the Spirit for community ministry?

nine

Finding Balance

In November 2014, the Discovery Channel aired a special called *Skywalker Live* featuring tightrope walker Nik Wallenda. Wallenda, a seventh-generation aerialist, was attempting to tightrope between two Chicago skyscrapers at a height of six hundred feet. To help wrap your mind around the height, that's as high as two football fields are long. That's pretty far up there! To top it off, he didn't use a net, and he was blindfolded. While walking six hundred feet above ground, blindfolded, with no net and his balancing pole firmly in hand, he somehow could hear the roaring of the crowd. In response to the crowd's applause, Wallenda said from his midair stage, "I love Chicago, and Chicago definitely loves me. What an amazing roar!"

Now, I love my community here in Portland, but there's no way I would ever place myself on a narrow rope fifty feet above ground, let alone six hundred feet. It wouldn't matter if someone offered me a million bucks—I wouldn't do it! But if you are serving your community in some way, you do have some Wallenda in your blood, because long-term and effective ministry to your community requires you to do a balancing act. Without balance in your life and ministry, you will fall off, burn out, quit and never make it to the other end of the rope.

Walking the Tightrope

A few years back, an older gentleman named Mr. Smith became part of our Life Change community. At first the dude seemed a little quirky. A large part of this quirkiness was the way he talked. He'd make a statement that he believed to be profound, and then he'd make a faint humming noise and peer into your eyes for a few uncomfortable seconds to make sure you were getting the message. Everyone has their quirks, including me, but his were more obvious than most.

After he had attended the church for about a year, he and I had a very transparent conversation. I discovered that he had served as a pastor in California and that his church had a very extensive ministry to the community. They fed, clothed, advocated for and shared Jesus with the community. It took me a minute to wrap my mind around his story, which was hard to believe at first. I was thinking, *Mr. Smith, what happened to you?* I wasn't planning to ask that question, but he answered it: "Mark, the ministry was going beautifully, but I got burned out and crashed." In other words, Mr. Smith fell off the rope.

The reality is that any of us can fall off the rope. The contrary winds of our community and our human frailties make us all susceptible to a crash. Finding balance and keeping balance is critical if you are going to facilitate Jesus collisions in your community.

Many tightrope walkers use a balancing pole—a long rod weighted at both ends so that the pole bends downward, forming a bow shape. Many think the only purpose of the pole is to lower the tightrope walker's center of gravity, which it does. However, the primary purpose of the pole is to increase the moment of inertia. The longer pole gives walkers more time to adjust to movements or rotations that would affect their balance. So instead of having half a second to respond to a wind gust, they have 1.5 seconds. The pole gives them the ability to feel and respond to the dislodging forces before they become overpowering.

Over the years, I've had many people who walk the tightrope of community ministry give me good tips on how to keep my balance. Many times I've been on the rope, shaking like a leaf in the wind, and the advice I've received has been very helpful to me. That collective wisdom has been my balancing pole, the pole I hold tightly in my heart and my hands to stay balanced regardless of the wind, missteps or vertigo. Let me share a few of these balancing gems to help keep you on the community tightrope.

Combat Stress

To say that ministry to a community can be stormy at times is a gross understatement. The winds of stress can cause the best of us to fall headlong off the high wire. You can't stay tensed up all the time, like an overwound clock. For your own health, you have to have fun from time to time to release the tension.

One of my former seminary professors told me he had two groups of friends when he was in seminary. One group consisted of serious-minded students that feverishly devoted all their time to academics and nothing else. They had no time for play. The other group studied hard but took the time to joke around, play Ping-Pong and enjoy life. Years after they had all graduated, the only ones left in ministry were those who knew how to have a little fun and a good laugh.

What are things you like to do for fun and enjoyment? Do them! Put them on your schedule just like you do your community ministry times. Not only that, be spontaneous from time to time. Do something wild and crazy that brings joy and happiness to your soul. Maybe you like to

- knit
- go to the movies
- play golf
- ride a horse
- talk politics
- take long walks
- paint
- go to museums or zoos

Whatever it is within the boundaries of God's Word, go for it!

I took up playing the bass recently, and I love it. I told myself that if I stuck with it for more than a year or two, I would buy myself (wife willing) a nice bass. I reached my goal and recently purchased a Fender American Jazz bass with a light wood body—absolutely beautiful!

When I play that instrument, I'm like a kid in a candy store. The *boom boom* thundering from the amp drowns out all the demands and needs of the church and community momentarily. While my fingers are on those strings, I'm in dreamland—at least until my wife comes downstairs and tells me, "Honey, turn that thing down! You're shaking the whole house." True, the house does shake sometimes, but I sure have fun rockin' the house. Not like I'm your dad or something, but I hereby grant you permission to have fun.

Find Rest

Rest is crucial in helping you maintain your balance. You know firsthand the difficulty of trying to function after a terrible night's sleep. You can't think straight, you're groggy and dizzy, and you slur like a pirate who found the captain's private reserve. It's a major task trying to stay on your feet tired.

You need times of rest. And God himself rested. He worked six days, and on the seventh day he rested, calling it the Sabbath. God's intention for us is not to be human-doings twenty-four hours a day, seven days a week. Before he made us to *do*, he made us to *be*. Being requires you and me to have time just to be, and that is called rest.

About twenty years ago at a leadership conference I attended, Rick Warren made a statement about rest I have never forgotten. He said that each of us should divert daily, withdraw weekly and abandon annually. Diverting daily means each day you deliberately focus your attention momentarily on something other than the grind of your tasks. For example, if your ministry is providing care and support to hurting families in your community, don't stay in that vortex all day long. Open the door and step out. Let your thoughts, actions and emotions focus on anything that's not job related.

Our church used to have a standing joke about where I was. If anyone would ask, the staff would laugh and say, "Guess." The right answer to the question was almost always Saigon Kitchen. On my birthday, they gave me a gift certificate to Saigon Kitchen, and they thought the gesture was absolutely hilarious. From my point of view, it was, "Thank you, Jesus, for such a great gift!" For me, a trip to Saigon Kitchen was a great daily diversion. Almost every day of the week I would meet my buddy George, and we would spend the hour talking about sports, finances and how good the noodles were.

Withdrawing weekly is fulfilling the command to take a weekly sabbath. It's a day when you rest. That means no calls, texts or anything else that is a part of your workflow. Man, I tell you, taking a weekly sabbath can be a challenge. The temptation is always present to get something done. When you work in the community, your work is never done. Taking a weekly sabbath rest helps to renew your strength and resolve. Not only that, it shows reliance on God to help with the work, because you understand that God is working even while you are resting. It also helps you to develop the ability to live with unfinished work, a quality that is of great importance when working in your community. What day do you take your sabbath?

Abandoning annually is about taking an extended break once a year. It doesn't have to be some expensive vacation. However, it does require an intentional get-out-of-Dodge move on your part. Schedule a week or two when you are, in essence, stranded on a desert island where no one who will put a demand on your time can reach you. A sign should be posted on your window for all to read: "Sorry, closed for business until . . ." If you don't take the initiative, no one else will do it for you. Getting the rest you need is important; make no apologies for taking it.

Hang Out with Jesus

The Twenty-Third Psalm talks about an incredible shepherd: Jesus. It expresses the wonderful care he provides for his sheep—that means you! Jesus, being the good Shepherd, promises that every need you have or will encounter he is able to meet. Listen to how the psalmist says the Lord cares for him:

- He provides him with a place where he can lie down and rest (v. 2).

- He satisfies his deepest thirsts (v. 2).

- He restores his soul (v. 3).

- He guides him in the right direction (v. 3).
- He provides him with constant companionship (v. 4).
- He gives him comfort (v. 4).
- He gives him victory over his enemies (v. 5).
- He blesses his entire life (v. 6).
- He gives him a place to dwell for eternity (v. 6).

As you serve your community, your shepherd desperately wants to care for you. Sure, he is sovereign and can do anything, but to be a recipient of his loving care, it helps for us to stay very close to him. The Bible tells us that Jesus often withdrew to lonely places and prayed. For him, being alone in his Father's presence was invaluable. In the intimacy of those moments, the Father was a shepherd to his Son, giving him everything he needed to fulfill his mission. Jesus often made decisions to spend time in his Father's presence, and we would be wise to do the same.

There is nothing like being in the presence of Jesus and allowing his grace and mercy to cover your entire being with his amazing love. Set aside a time in the day when you can have time alone with Jesus. My time is in the morning. I love to get in the presence of Jesus before the noise of the day begins. During that time, I pour my heart out to God in prayer and then receive from him the grace I need to make it through the day. I cannot tell you how many times my soul has wobbled, and I have felt myself slipping off my rope, only to have my equilibrium restored in the presence of Jesus. William Walford had it right when he penned these hymn lyrics back in the 1800s:

Sweet hour of prayer! Sweet hour of prayer!
That calls me from a world of care,
And bids me at my Father's throne

Make all my wants and wishes known.
In seasons of distress and grief,
My soul has often found relief,
And oft escaped the tempter's snare,
By thy return, sweet hour of prayer!

The morning time is great, but don't limit your time with Jesus to a certain time and place. Hang out with him everyplace and all day. Morning, noon and evening, pray to him. From the rising of the sun until it goes down, praise him. If you hang out with Jesus, he will make your feet like a hind's feet, and you will walk the community tightrope well.

Don't Cage Your Feelings

The first time I preached in Brazil, I was amazed by the weather. One minute, torrential rain was pouring down, flooding the streets. The next minute, the sun was blazing in full glory. It was two extremes. Ministry to the community can seem that way at times. One minute you're on cloud nine, and the next minute you're deep in the abyss.

Our 11:45 outreach works with the police bureau and other agencies to curb gang violence. For three years, we had people in bright green T-shirts walking in the Albina-Killingsworth District, talking with people and praying with them on occasion. These walkers were grandmas, businesspeople and average Joes. They developed beautiful relationships with people as well as the college and businesses in the area.

As a result of the collaborative efforts of many groups, including our own, during those three years, the crime rate dropped by 30 percent, and no shootings took place. This information was given to us during a meeting at our church with about fifteen to twenty leaders and officials present. The police commander said we should be proud of the good work we had done together and should feel pretty special as a result. We applauded and were grateful for the decrease in crime—and most of all for no shootings. We were all on cloud nine, knowing our hard work had paid off.

But that celebration was short lived. The very next day, four kids in that area were shot in front of an alternative high school. One day we were celebrating a documented victory and first thing the next day, four kids were shot. Fortunately, all of them recovered.

Chances are, you won't be involved in this type of community work, but maybe you will. But this story applies to other types of ministry. What happens when you help get a marriage on the right track, only to discover several months down the road that the couple got a divorce? Or maybe you're involved in a group with businesspeople, pouring your heart out in talks about doing business with integrity, only to find out that one of the people you thought was honest got busted for illegal activity. Community work can put you on a rollercoaster of emotions.

I've received wise advice: Cry when you need to, and celebrate when you need to. Don't try to be a he-man or a she-woman, bottling up all your disappointments and joys. Let them out! Express them to God and to others. You may not change the situation, but at least you'll divert a brewing storm that could blow you off the wire. Listen, friend, no one will think less of you because you let your true colors show from time to time. In fact, others will probably appreciate you more for allowing them to see the true you.

Network

I've talked to dozens of people over the years that were excited about starting a new ministry to reach their community. As I listened to them enthusiastically telling me their dreams, I sometimes realized that someone else was already doing the ministry they were describing. So I'd say, "Hey, so-and-so, do you know that this other person is doing that same thing?" The responses varied. Some said, "Yes, but my ministry . . . " Others responded with a yes and were eager to connect with that other person to learn more or to see how they could help.

Ministry to community is not an island endeavor; you need others to help you. As I said earlier, God's plan is not for you to meet every need in your community alone, nor has he given you all the tools and gifts needed even to attempt such a feat. Whatever you or I do in our communities is only a small slice of the pie. And one sliver of pie can't feed an entire community.

The person who attempts to minister to his or her community without networking or partnering with like-minded individuals is trying to walk a tightrope with one foot. Ecclesiastes 4:9-12 expresses the benefit of networking and partnership:

Two are better than one,
    because they have a good return for their work:
If one falls down,
    his friend can help him up.
But pity the man who falls
    and has no one to help him up!
Also, if two lie down together, they will keep warm.
    But how can one keep warm alone?
Though one may be overpowered,
    two can defend themselves.
A cord of three strands is not quickly broken.

You know as well as I do that the little ego monster will raise up its prideful head to influence you to make your work a one-man or one-woman show. You inflate your chest to one hundred inches so that everyone can see what you're doing and what you've done. The problem with a one-person show is that it's always short lived. I've been on the block a few years, so I've seen my share of one-hit wonders come and go. They're serving today and gone tomorrow. They worked by themselves and fizzled out by themselves.

God wants whatever ministry you do in your community to be substantial, and he graciously gives you the gifts of other people to make that happen. If you take the time to build relationships and to network with other like-minded and like-hearted people, you will find great stability that will help you go the distance.

Stay Connected to Your Church

Avoid the trap of becoming so popular in the community that you become a stranger at church. The following example may stretch this idea a bit, but it illustrates the point. You've probably heard the story of PKs (pastor's kids) who are totally turned off of God because their dad spent a lot of time with the church and not enough at home. These kids are bitter, and eventually their anger takes a toll on their dad as well, causing him pain and regret over his absenteeism. The church is your home (again, I'm stretching this a bit). It's the place where your spiritual family meets to spend time with each other and your heavenly Father. When you are perpetually absent from your family, everyone is adversely affected.

Remember, part of reaching your community is proper positioning. Your right position is in a strategic place between the church and the community (Bethel and Ai). If you abandon the community of faith God has placed you in, you may become an outreach candidate (someone has to reach out and bring you back home). If you find yourself getting to a place where you're saying, "I haven't seen ... in such a long time," chances are you're losing your balance. If you reach a point where you don't care whether or not you've seen your church family in a while, you have indeed lost your balance.

To grow spiritually, you need the community of faith. You need your church for accountability and support. You need your church because it's God's idea, and because he says it's where he wants you to be. Yes, your community is important and needs you desperately, but your local church needs you too, and you need your local church. Stay connected not just with your body but with your heart as well. Hebrews 10:23-25 says it beautifully: "Let us hold unswervingly to the hope we profess, for he who promised is faithful. And let us consider how we may spur one another on toward love and good deeds. Let us not give up meeting together, as some are in the habit of doing, but let us encourage one another—and all the more as you see the Day approaching."

I have been disillusioned with the local church at times—and even frustrated to the hilt! Yes, at times I've felt like leaving the church. That said, I'm so thankful for the wise people over the years who have encouraged me to stay connected to the church. Much of the work I'm personally involved in with my community today started because I was a part of the church. Without the church, I doubt my life would have much community impact at all.

If you have an idea that the church doesn't embrace right away, don't become angry and leave. For one, your idea may not be something God wants the entire church to do; maybe he's talking just to you. Or there may be a lack of enthusiasm because God is still working character into your soul while simultaneously preparing others to participate in the outreach one day. God times all his plans perfectly, and giving in to a knee-jerk reaction by bolting out the door could abort the wonderful plan God has in store a few blocks down the road.

For Reflection and Discussion

1. What are some areas that you struggle with in terms of balancing life and ministry?

2. Was there a time when you fell off the tightrope? How did you regain your balance?

3. What do you do for fun? When do you get rest?

4. Have you been spending time hanging out with Jesus?

5. What is your plan to stay in balance?

6. How will you pray for yourself and your church to stay balanced in community life and church life?

ten

Super-Simple Plan

I enjoy preparing a good meal for my family, and I love to clown around while I'm doing it. For the hour or two that it takes me to make the meal, our kitchen transforms into my own television show, of which the star is none other than West Coast G. Garvin Jr.—who happens to be me—good ol' dad. I came up with the name G. Garvin Jr. because my favorite cooking show is *Turn up the Heat with G. Garvin.* Garvin is a great chef who cooks with an urban flare. His program is filled with energy; there's no slow, no monotone in his presentation. He talks about the food and its presentation with a contagious passion that, as my son would say, "gets me hyped."

Garvin has a few signature moves and sayings that I skillfully incorporated into my show. One is the pepper mill move. The way Garvin adds pepper to a dish is a fine art. He'll grab the tall pepper mill, place it over the pot and add the pepper. Each turn of the pepper mill is accentuated with a swift semi-twist of the shoulders like the munchkin twist in *The Wizard of Oz.* And the shoulder move is emphasized by a verbal "Ah . . . ah!" Once the pepper is added, he says his tag line: "It's super-simple— super-simple."

My family gets a big kick out of my cooking show. In fact, they gave me a G. Garvin cookbook for Christmas, and they bought me my own pepper mill out of the blue. When I'm in the kitchen, they just laugh and shake their heads. When I'm deep in my alter ego, my daughter McKenzie always says, "Dad, you think you are G. Garvin!" To which I reply, "It's super-simple—super-simple!" Then, with one of those big McKenzie smiles, she shakes her head and walks off saying, "Just let me know when it's time to eat."

You're probably asking about now, "Mark, what in the world do your cooking show fantasies have to do with me impacting my community?" Not much. But G. Garvin's cooking philosophy is extremely helpful for us when it comes to formulating our plan to merge with our community. Our plan has to be super-simple—super-simple!

Even though you may deal with some very complex community issues, a super-simple plan is a great tool to help you get the job done. We've seen God accomplish some phenomenal things in our community as a result of the execution of such a plan.

One day a friend of mine was looking at the Columbia River when he noticed rows of large waves rippling out from where he was. He thought a boat or even a barge was creating the disturbance. On closer observation, he discovered it was a duck creating all of those waves. That's the kind of impact a simple plan can have in your community: it can create some huge wakes.

11:45

What God has accomplished through 11:45 in our community is more than any of us imagined or dreamed. It's also an excellent example of how a super-simple plan can have a great impact on a complex issue affecting your community. We never thought that we would

- be a part of a collaboration that caused a 34.4 percent decrease in misdemeanor crimes and a 67 percent decrease in violent crimes;

- sign up the largest number of mentors to serve Big Brothers Big Sisters at one time in the state of Oregon—and receive national attention for doing so;

- be welcomed in our local mall to walk and converse with shoppers and even pray with some, let alone be appreciated for our service;

- work in close association with the district attorney's office, judges, the city and the police department and have monthly meetings with them at the church where we express our faith freely and pray openly;

- impact our city from the street level to the government level;

- have the opportunity to pray for large numbers of hurting people on the streets and even prevent some from committing suicide;

- impact other cities, both rural and urban, to the degree that they would visit us and look for ways to adapt our model to their city;

- impact gentrification issues in our community and have an influence on how the city would spend more than $20 million to help the disenfranchised with housing;

- be the first faith-based outreach to receive a Police Medal of Accommodation for community service and the mayor's Spirit Award for service to the community;

- sit in a community meeting and hear individuals publicly state how 11:45's services changed the way they view the church;
- serve and love our community for Jesus; or
- see people come to faith in Christ and be baptized.

I could go on, but you get the point. God can accomplish great things if you have a super-simple plan.

Crafting Your Plan

I'm sure you've heard this old adage before: "To fail to plan is to plan to fail." You cannot afford to fail, because your community is waiting for you, and your community needs you.

To craft a super-simple plan, you only need to answer four easy questions:

1. What is your mission?
2. What steps are needed to accomplish your mission?
3. How will you hold yourself accountable?
4. How will you evaluate your progress?

By answering these questions, you will have a super-simple plan for community action.

Question 1: What is your mission? Asking what your mission is helps answer the question, What does God want me to do in my community? There are definitely a lot of things you could do, but what is the *one* thing God is asking of you? That's what you've got to nail down. To answer this question, consider your passion. What is the area of community need that makes your heart jump? Where is the place you see the greatest need? Once you identify that, ask yourself, What is the one thing I can do to work toward reducing that need?

For 11:45, our goal was to curb the wave of gang violence. Our team discerned that God's plan for us was to use our position as pastors to mobilize the church for community action. We figured if we could rally followers of Jesus Christ from our churches around stopping community violence, we could make a difference. So our answer to "what do you want to do?" was to mobilize one hundred people from Portland-area churches to volunteer—for one year, once a week for forty-five minutes (hence 11:45)—to serve in four strategic areas (There-Share-Care-Prayer) to aid existing city and community efforts in stopping gang violence and its aftermath on our streets. In a nutshell, our mission and goal was the following:

- Engage the church in being part of a solution to help solve the gang violence problem.

- Engage one hundred volunteers to serve at a doable commitment level.

- Give the volunteers an opportunity to serve in one of four service areas.

That's all we believed God wanted us to do. Simple, right?

Question 2: What steps are needed to accomplish your mission? To craft your plan, you need to identify and list all the steps necessary for accomplishing your mission. The steps you define will give you a clear path for action and execution. For 11:45, there were several initial steps we had to take. First, we had to figure out how we could recruit and inspire people to volunteer. Second, we had to give a crystal-clear invitation to serve and give volunteers an open path for service. To accomplish this goal, we decided to have a community meeting to which every church in our community was invited. At the gathering, community leaders discussed the problem, and then we invited people to serve, giving them a clear path to take to get involved.

On that night, we accomplished those two objectives. The mayor came and spoke about the problem, as did several community advocates. Then we shared how people could volunteer and make a difference. We gave them four options:

1. They could be a part of the There Team, which is a loving, visible presence. This group of volunteers would walk areas that we call "Hot Spots," places where problematic activity could happen. This group would just walk in those areas and love on people.

2. They could be a part of the Share Team, being a connecting presence. This group would pair up children who needed mentoring through Big Brothers Big Sisters.

3. They could be a part of the Care Team, being a supporting presence. This group would show the love of Jesus to families that were hurting due to violence.

4. They could be a part of the Prayer Team, being an interceding presence. This group would meet once a month to pray for the issues and all who were working on the front lines.

We designated four areas in the church, one for each of the serving components, and we encouraged people to go to the area where they had the most interest. In each one of those areas, we gave more information regarding the responsibilities and the purpose of that ministry focus. We articulated how important each person was in reaching our community and then asked all who were interested to sign the roster. Those who signed were given places, dates and times when they were needed to volunteer.

Our kickoff meeting went great. Our goal was to enlist one hundred volunteers, but God, by his grace, gave us four hundred. We also had a good number of people sign up for every team. We were totally jazzed, and so was everyone present.

To sum up our steps, we

- organized a kickoff rally that brought the church community together and created awareness of the need, giving the church an opportunity to be a part of the solution;

- clearly presented a pathway for community service by making sure people understood there were four ways they could participate: There, Share, Care, or Prayer; and

- got people to sign up and gave them their marching orders that night.

Once we identified the primary steps, all we had to do was fill in the logistical blanks to make it happen. Figure out the big steps first, and attend to the smaller details once you figure the path that will get you where you want to go.

Question 3: How will you hold yourself accountable? Accountability is important no matter how trustworthy you are. It is a wise mechanism to build into your plan to help ensure your missional success. Accountability helps keep you on the right track and guards you from blind spots you may have. We built accountability into multiple levels of 11:45.

First, we have our mission statement and objectives. Our goal is to help youth, work for a safer city and merge the church with the community in order to share Christ. This means that if we get an offer to start selling paintbrushes, we have to turn down that opportunity because it is not in line with our mission.

Second, six key pastors meet together weekly. Those relationships help keep our community focus on track. I can't tell you how many discussions we've had on what to do and what not do as it pertains to our mission.

Third, we have the M&Ms: Marcie Spruill and Marcie Jackson. These two wise, competent women are part of our team, where they act as compasses to hold us in line with our God-given mission. We respect their voices and listen to what they have to say.

You may not need a whole group of people to hold you accountable in your mission. Your friend, spouse or anyone you know that will tell you the truth will work just fine. It doesn't have to be complicated. Just find one or two people who will help you remain true to what God has called you to and to what you said you are going to do.

Question 4: How will you evaluate your progress? Evaluation is not about how many and how much. In Christendom we are prone to declare something a success or a failure based on how many people we reach and how much money we acquire. If money and bodies were the total sum of our evaluation, a lot of Jesus' choicest followers would be considered failures.

Sure, there is a place for evaluating with numbers—for examples, see the book of Numbers and the book of Acts. There are even accounts in the Bible of how many people Jesus fed and healed in a single setting. But that's not the whole ball of wax. Jesus said, "I only do what I see my Father doing" (John 5:19, paraphrase). That's called faithfulness.

At the end of day, you have to answer a few questions: Am I being faithful to the task God has given me to carry out in my community? Is there something I can do to fulfill my task more effectively? Is there anything God wants me to add or subtract? Evaluation removes the luxury of placing the mission on autopilot and never checking with God to see if you need to change course.

Once every couple of months, all of the 11:45 pastors meet to pray with one another for the purpose of building relationships and evaluating where we are on our community journey. We want to quiet our hearts together before the Lord to hear how he says it's going. We also look at our volunteer numbers and financial needs and then plan how to act accordingly. Our primary goal, though, is to check in with Jesus to see how he says we are doing. (Yes, he will let you know, if you ask.)

Here are a couple of evaluation tips:

- If you keep records, pay attention to what they are telling you. Be wise and make adjustments as needed.

- Ask yourself how you are doing in relationship building. Community is all about relationships. Maybe there are certain people that need a little more time with you. Or perhaps you struggle in a relational area, and you need to acquire tools to help you grow. Or you may be doing great and need to give yourself a big pat on the back.

- Spend time with God. If God was faithful to put you into your community ministry, God will be faithful to help you evaluate your progress along the way. Put a date on the calendar when you will talk with the Lord specifically about how you're doing.

Back to "It's super-simple—super-simple!" Again, by answering these four questions, you will have crafted your simple strategy to make some big waves in your community.

1. What is your mission?

2. What steps are needed to accomplish your mission?

3. How will you hold yourself accountable?

4. How will you evaluate your progress?

The church is made for a merger with the community, and you are a part of the church. Your community is waiting for you to break out and meet them at the threshold. Jesus is waiting for you to break out too, so that he can go with you and create a collision in your community that will transform lives.

Now is the time to get moving! You're positioned correctly, and you have a super-simple strategy that's primed for action. Now is the time to make the merger and create a Jesus collision in your community. Let's go, church! The community is waiting for us.

For Reflection and Discussion

1. What is your mission?

2. What are the steps needed to accomplish your mission?

3. How will you hold yourself accountable?

4. How will you evaluate your progress?

5. What is your strategy for praying for a divine merger in your community?

Notes

Chapter 1: Strategic Positioning

[1]John H. Walton, Victor H. Matthews and Mark W. Chavalas, "Genesis 12:9," in *The IVP Bible Background Commentary: Old Testament*, electronic ed. (Downers Grove, IL: InterVarsity Press, 2000).

[2]D. A. Carson, "Matthew," in *The Expositor's Bible Commentary*, vol. 8, *Matthew, Mark, Luke*, ed. F. E. Gaebelein (Grand Rapids: Zondervan, 1984), 140.

Chapter 4: Presenting an Authentic Jesus

[1]Ronald J. Sider, Philip N. Olson and Heidi Rolland Unruh, *Churches That Make a Difference: Reaching Your Community with Good News and Good Works*, Kindle ed. (Grand Rapids: Baker Books, 2002), loc. 66-69.

[2]"Wishful Thinking Quotes," Good Reads, www.goodreads.com/work /quotes/118728-wishful-thinking-a-seeker-s-abc.

Chapter 8: Depending on the Spirit

[1]Cornelia Seigneur, "100 Men Standing Against Portland's Gangs," *Christianity Today*, November 30, 2011, www.christianitytoday.com/thisisourcity /portland/portlandsgangs.html?paging=off.

Also Available by Mark E. Strong

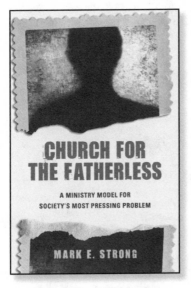

Church for the Fatherless
978-0-8308-3790-8